LIVE LIKE YOU MEAN IT

S. JAMES MEYER

Live Like You Mean It

REIMAGINING YOUR *purpose* AND *vocation*

TWENTY-THIRD PUBLICATIONS

twentythirdpublications.com

Twenty-Third Publications
977 Hartford Turnpike Unit A
Waterford, CT 06385
(860) 437-3012 or (800) 321-0411
twentythirdpublications.com

Cover photo: Photocreo Bednarek – stock.adobe.com

ISBN: 978-1-62785-799-4
Printed in the U.S.A.

 A division of Bayard, Inc.

Meaning
is not always
something we
get
from life,

Often, it's
something
we're meant
to
bring
to life.

CONTENTS

FIRST THINGS FIRST:

Pursue Purpose, Not Problems

I GET LOST A LOT. MOSTLY IT'S BECAUSE MY MIND IS OFF ON ITS OWN JOURNEY, AND I FOLLOW IT. I'll blow past freeway exits, take wrong turns, and go on obliviously for miles. I even missed a turn on my way to church one morning along a very short route I had traveled hundreds of times. At one point, my wife and kids turned their frustrations into entertainment by keeping a log in the glovebox to record my errant turns. When the whole family was in the car together, they'd break it out and read each other's recent entries. Yes, there were always recent entries. Sometimes daily, always weekly. I get lost a lot.

Getting lost used to be annoying and stressful, but now I regard it as interesting. "I think you were supposed to turn back there," Michelle will say. "Huh," I'll respond. "I guess we're off on an adventure now."

I've seen, discovered, and stumbled upon a lot of cool places as a result of this. Through it all, three valuable life lessons have emerged: 1) I never know where lost will lead; 2) Most of the time, I'm not lost at all. I'm just suddenly on a different course; 3) I'm going to find my way eventually, so I might as well enjoy the ride.

Getting lost is a pretty good metaphor for how I've journeyed through my whole life. I've been making this whole thing up as I go. Whenever I would miss a turn, one of my kids would ask, "Do you even know where you're going, Dad?" The answer always was and still is no. No, I don't know where I'm going. Geographically, in the moment, sure. Kind of. Usually. But overall in life? No. I have no cosmic GPS. There's no Google Maps voice in my ear telling me I'm on the fastest route or that I should drive straight for seven miles and keep left at the fork. Arguably, I'm joyriding my way through life, navigating only by faith.

And you know what? I am extremely and quite accidentally happy. There have been very difficult and challenging days along the way, and I've taken more than my share of wrong turns. I've had to negotiate twists, turmoil, and detours I never saw coming, and I've sat up at night feeling very lost and alone. Through it all, though, my life has been fulfilling beyond my dreams, and I am overcome with joy and gratitude.

I have no idea what the meaning of my life is, but I absolutely know my life is and has been deeply meaningful, not only for myself but for others as well. None of it was planned. In fact, it was all very intentionally unplanned. There were no goal-setting retreats, no vision boards, master plans, or mind maps, and no timelines. Some might think this approach has been irresponsible, but I'll argue that the most responsible thing I've ever done was accept that I'm not the best one to be in charge of my life.

I distinctly remember the night I did not plan any of it—an unseasonably warm Saturday in early April. I was twenty-two, a college senior, walking home from my girlfriend's house sometime after midnight. The moon was near full, and the spring air blew the scent of impending graduation into my face. I sneezed violently as with an allergy. The thought was ominous and haunting. Graduation was five weeks away and I had no plan. Zero. The job market for freelance philosophers, wannabe poets, and young men with opinions was not exactly robust.

Lost, clueless, and searching, I approached a church I had passed a hundred times before but had never been inside. This time I paused and stared at the oversized wooden doors. Surely, they would be locked at this hour. Feeling pulled toward a sanctuary and away from my own anxiety, I ascended the concrete steps. It's safe to approach a locked church—there's no real commitment. As I pulled on one of the large iron handles, the door responded surprisingly, opening silently and softly.

Slipping into a back pew, I simply sat and breathed. There, in the dark silence, I prayed and waited. And prayed and waited. And waited. Nothing happened. The statues didn't start weeping. The candles didn't start flickering. The shadows didn't spell out messages. I was looking for a sign, a symbol, some sort of indication that I would be ok, something—anything—to give me direction. Nothing

3

happened. There would be no miracles that night, real or imagined.

Finally, I got up and said out loud, "OK, God. If you're not going to tell me what to do or where to turn, I guess I'll just wander blindly. Nudge me if and when I need to zig or zag." That was it. Then I left.

Back on the sidewalk and looking up at the stars, I was struck with a reassuring sense that although I felt lost and confused, I was on the right track, walking the path I needed to walk. It was then that I added these words to my prayer, words I have uttered nearly every day since, "OK, God, we have an understanding then—you lead, I'll follow, and I don't need to know where we're going." That's when my joyride really started.

All these decades later, I find myself transitioning into my fourth vocation. None of it has been planned. God led. I followed. And I still don't know where this life is headed. My vocations have been cumulative, stacking up in ways that make my life experience ever richer and ever more meaningful. My first vocation was and is marriage and parenthood. What a wild and joyful ride that has been, and I now add to it my role as a grandparent. There has been so much love and so much meaning! It blows my mind, and I feel as though I've ascended into paradise without ever having to die.

My second vocation has been as a leader and contributor in business. I have used my talents to lead teams of people in efforts to serve and support organizations that are doing good things in the world. Every day in my professional career has been motivated by this purpose: put something good in the world that wasn't there before.

My third vocation has been that of diaconal ministry. As an ordained deacon I have helped build street-level outreach ministries that feed the hungry and shelter the homeless. I've been blessed to journey alongside people through major life events, such as weddings, baptisms, and funerals. What a gift I've been given by people who have opened their vulnerabilities and let me inside! Like Thomas in the gospel, I've had so many questions and doubts along the way, and all these images of Christ have opened their wounds to my hands so I could believe.

"OK, God... you lead, I'll follow, and I don't need to know where we're going."

Now I'm hitting a stride in my fourth vocation as an author, writing books that hopefully inspire people and communities whom I will never have the privilege of meeting. I have found this work to be deeply and profoundly meaningful as I hear from so many seekers and searchers looking for a pragmatic, down-to-earth spirituality with which they can laugh and cry. I now open my own wounds and vulnerabilities to all of you.

The point of sharing all this is to illustrate just how powerful and meaningful life can be even when you have no idea where you're going. But there is one catch: you have to open yourself to possibility and purpose. You have to decide that you will focus on possibility rather than problems. It's not unlike my experience of getting lost. I can choose to see it as being a problem, or I can choose to see it as opening new possibilities.

To help, let me first assure you that your life has purpose. You might not be Jesus, here to save all of humanity, but you are still here on this life journey to do something, learn something, or touch someone. Your life matters. I'm willing to wager that you already believe this, you sense it, but it still feels good to hear someone else say it objectively. Your life has purpose. Breathe deeply and let that thought fill your lungs. Sit with it a bit. Learn to trust it. Your life has significance and has been given to you as a gift to share.

Whatever your purpose might be in the long run, it is bigger than you are. It is bigger than your ego, deeper than your fears, and broader than your comfort zones. This is true regardless of your age or life stage, whether you are anxious about acne or aching with arthritis. Along life's path thus far, you have most likely invested much spiritual and mental energy attempting to figure this all out, seeking to understand why you are here and what it means. But there are no rational answers to spiritual questions. The meaning of your life, like love itself, cannot be known; it can only be experienced and shared.

Regardless of the circumstances that brought you into this world, and regardless of the difficulties and challenges you might currently face, your life in this time and place is intentional and purposeful. In this moment, you are exactly where you need to be on your journey toward wholeness, with an understanding that you will grow forward from here. You are an important part of a mystery far bigger and far greater than any of us by ourselves.

With all my heart and soul, I believe you are a life force and a love force, created in the image and likeness of a Creator I won't pretend to understand, a Creator who is the source of all life and love. Even if you're rolling your eyes right now thinking I'm some sort of religious zealot who is a few beads short of a full rosary, and even if you are not sure what (or if) you believe about God, you are still a life force and a love force in the universe. You are able to bring hope, joy, compassion, and kindness into the world. And that is gobsmacking amazing!

I'm being careful not to say your life has "A" purpose, because I don't know that. Maybe it does. Who am I to say otherwise? But there's a good chance your life's purpose might not be simple or singular. It probably isn't obvious. It's likely an unfolding mystery that you continue to pursue even though you don't yet see or understand it.

There's something else worth putting on your radar here: meaning and purpose do not dull or diminish with age. I learned this from my father in his dying days, a last gift from him. Even when he had let go of everything else— including independence, dignity, the ability to speak and feed himself—and he was on the threshold of letting go of this life itself, he still shared love, joy, and peace in a brilliant, cut-through way. In his very last days, he moved me, my mother, and my siblings in a way that forever changed us. His life and death were gifts that made our hearts bigger.

If your life's purpose is singular and/or is clear to you, I hope you are living with deep gratitude and appreciation. You are among a very lucky (or unlucky?) few. The rest of us wander, search, and even flounder as we try our best to make sense of things. I have met a few people along life's journey who are confident they have it figured out. God bless 'em, I guess. I wonder, though, if they're not missing out on the rich joy of the pilgrimage.

I offer this book to you as a pilgrim's guide of sorts. When I look at the world around me, I see so many people who are struggling to find footing, who are growing cynical at what strikes them as the futility of life. It doesn't have to be that way, and they don't realize they have a choice. Again, you can choose to focus on purpose or on problems. When you choose purpose, you are ready to live like you mean it.

1

The Search for Wisdom and Meaning

HELENA BJORKMAN HAD BEEN CAMERA SHY HER ENTIRE LIFE. Even as a child, she avoided the spotlight and didn't like being the center of attention. Others found this odd since her very presence radiated a natural essence that every lens loved. There had never been anything particular about her features to define her beauty, but there was certainly something about her. Whenever she was included in a group photo, such as her high school forensics team or class confirmation photo, hers was the first face people noticed, and even as they looked at the others, their eyes kept going back to her. People gravitated toward her without knowing why. She was typically quiet and a bit shy, with a heart that seemed to express itself through her kind, gentle eyes. This is what people noticed, although they didn't realize it. And they couldn't look away.

Now, decades later and in her seventies, Helena still doesn't like cameras, and she wants no part of social media. "Attention is a gift of great value when given, but of no value when received," she told her grandson Max, who was following her around the kitchen with his iPhone, recording everything she said.

"It means a lot to me that you're doing this, Grandma. I know you don't like it, but it's for school. It's an assignment."

"You're thirteen years old. You're perfectly capable of being annoying without the job being assigned as a school project." Her wide smile and the lilt in her voice assured Max she was just teasing. She set a plate of cookies on the table and sat down. "Well, let's get on with it, then. We'll talk until these cookies are gone, and I'm only eating one, so you'd better get crackin' or you'll be late for soccer practice."

"Grandma," Max said as he focused his phone on her seasoned face, "who is the wisest person you ever met?"

The older woman wrapped both hands around her coffee mug and stared at the ceiling for a bit. "You know, Max, sadly, I haven't met a lot of people who I would say are wise. There are a lot of people who know a lot of things, or at least think they do, but there are very few who are truly wise. There's a big difference between knowledge and wisdom, and I'd say right now the world needs a lot more wisdom to catch up with all the knowledge."

She paused and let that hang in the air. Max looked a little perplexed, and she realized her answer wasn't all that helpful. It was more theoretical than concrete, and seventh graders need things to be concrete. She continued, "But I have been blessed to have known a few very wise people. The wisest, I'd say, would have been your Great

Grandfather and my father-in-law, Anders Bjorkman. I think one of the reasons I married your grandpa Lars was that he was so heavily influenced by the wisdom of his own father." She fidgeted with her thin, gold wedding band as she spoke, recalling that it was the same ring Anders had given to his wife, who would have been her mother-in-law had she lived. For a moment she lost herself in thought about how our lives are touched by people we never meet. She chose her words carefully, fully aware that she was now a conduit through which Max's life was being touched by Anders Bjorkman, a man she grew to love and respect, but whom Max would never know personally. "Anders had a thoughtful and measured way about him," she continued. "He was a deep-thinking Christian man, and whenever there was a tough decision to make, he'd lean back in his chair, take a deep drag on his pipe, and then he'd slowly say, 'Well, commit your error on the side of compassion.' That's wise advice; words to live by."

Max turned the camera on himself to ask his follow-up. "What did he mean by that?"

"I think he meant that life is, well, it's often complicated. The road ahead is seldom clear. We have to make decisions without knowing what's best or sometimes even knowing what's right. The wise person, Anders would say, always chooses the most compassionate option."

"How do you know what's most compassionate?" Max asked as he shoved a cookie in his mouth with one hand while keeping his phone pointed with the other. "Sorry about the crumbs. I'm not good at eating with my left hand."

"Compassion isn't something we can know. It's something we must feel. So, it doesn't help to think about it; we have to contemplate it. Meditate on it. You really have to get in touch with your soul to discern which path is the most loving, and even then it won't necessarily be clear." Recognizing that wheels were turning inside her grandson's head, Helena made up an excuse about needing to check the dryer so he would have a little space to process his thoughts.

> It's funny how the spirit works. We think we're giving others what they need, and we end up getting what we need.

As she was leaving the room, Max called out, "Grandma, while you're doing that, would you think about the next question: How does someone become wise?"

"Life was a lot easier," she called back, "when you just wanted to know where babies come from!" She had created some time and space for Max to ponder, but it turned out she needed it for herself. It's funny how the spirit works. We think we're giving others what they need, and we end up getting what we need. Usually, the return is not this immediate, but in this case, Helena was glad it was. She was seventy-one years old and was sure Max thought she was elderly. She was, after all, a card-carrying AARP member, and she had stopped dying her hair right about the time Max was born. Still, she didn't think of herself as old, not by a long shot. Sure, she didn't like social media, but that wasn't because she was old; it's because she thought it was an utter waste of time and energy. No, she wasn't old, but she did think of herself as having entered the wisdom stage of life, and now this thirteen-year-old kid was sitting in her kitchen expecting her to tell him in fifteen minutes what it took her a lifetime to discover—that wisdom starts when you stop thinking you have the answers. And he wanted answers. "Jesus, Joseph, and Mary," she whispered under her breath, "you'd better grab the helm and steer this submarine, because I'm in way over my head."

Helena returned to the room and sat down. "Listen," she said.

"OK," Max replied with his phone's lens fixed on her. "Go ahead. I'm listening."

"No," Helena responded. "I'm not asking you to listen, I'm telling you that listening is the answer. You asked how someone becomes wise, and that's the answer—they listen."

"Like to what? To music? Listen to music?"

"Yes, to music. But not just to the music; listen to the silence between the notes. Listen to the lyrics, the pauses, and the breaths. Listen to everything, Max. Listen to everything and to nothing. Listen to the sounds of the forest, the hush of the breeze, and the silence of the sunrise. Listen to the anxieties of the rich and the cries of the poor, to the giggles of small children and the creaking bones of the aged. Listen to all of it, but mostly listen to the whispers of the spirit inside you. If you want the gift of wisdom, then quiet the voices in your own head, turn down the volume of your own thoughts, and listen. Let the Creator speak to you through all of creation. Anders once told me that the reason there is so little wisdom in the world is because we are too preoccupied with the smallness between our own ears, so we never open ourselves to the greatness of God's infinite wholeness."

She took a ponderous sip of her coffee and a deep breath. "One time your grandpa Lars and I went up to see the northern lights, and while I was yammering on about how magnificent they are, he said, 'Shh, we can't listen to them if we're talking.' Anders had coached him from little on to listen to beauty."

Max jumped in, "Wait just a minute, Grandma. Were my Bjorkman ancestors into magic mushrooms or something? How do you listen to light and color? There is no sound."

"A wise person's experience is not limited by the laws of physics, Max. Hearing and listening are two different things. We hear sound, but we listen to meaning. And you can't listen with the ears on your head, you must listen with what Saint Benedict called the ear of the heart." She looked into his eyes to read whether any of this was registering. Max had brown eyes like his mother, but they were deep and penetrating like his grandfather's. It struck her that he was gifted with the dimensional vision of a sage, able to see both the surface and the depths of life. This would prove useful over the years ahead, but he would need to learn great patience and forgiveness lest he grow cynical. For now, still in the morning sunlight of youthful innocence, he was completely unaware of this gift. He hadn't walked through life's desert yet. That would come in its own time, and she was responsible for preparing him to face the trials and temptations he, like all of us, would face. "Hearing happens in the connections between our ears and our brains," she clarified. "It's physical and neurological. But listening happens in the connection between our minds and our souls, a connection that travels straight through our hearts. It's spiritual. So, you see, when we love, we listen; and when we listen, we grow in love. They go together. We struggle with this because we're enamored with our own thoughts; we don't ever get out of our own heads. How will you ever carry peace into another person's heart if you can't get out of your own head?"

Max set down his phone and held his head in both hands. This was more than he had signed up for, but he had no desire to back out. He wanted to go deeper. "That's a lot to think about, Grandma. I'm trying to listen, but there's not enough sugar in all these cookies to get my brain up to speed with yours."

Helena smiled at the young man who was discovering mystery for the first time but was still under the illusion that all mysteries can be solved by the time a movie ends. How do you tell a curious thirteen-year-old that questions have more value than answers—that questions keep drawing you deeper into mystery, but answers cause you to stop searching? How do you tell someone who is excited about figuring out life that, like God and love, life is not something we can ever know or understand; it's something we can only embrace and experience, but that's far more rewarding?

"Often the best way to get your mind up to speed is to slow down your brain," she said.

"Aren't they the same thing, your brain and your mind? How can I accelerate my mind by slowing down my brain? Isn't that like saying I can drive faster by slowing down the car?"

"Your analogy holds up, Max, only if the sole purpose for driving the car is to arrive at a destination. But what if you are in the car with family or friends? What if the purpose of driving the car is to journey together? Or to appreciate the marvel of the car's engineering? Or to have some alone time and listen to a podcast or an audio book? Or just to contemplate the beauty of the nature you're driving through? In all those cases, you can accelerate deeper into your real purpose by slowing down. Going fast is counterproductive."

"I get impatient in the car, and my dad keeps telling me that the journey is the reward. Is this what he means?"

"I would think so, yes. Life isn't about function, Max. It's about experience. It's about growth, discovery, and relationships. Do you remember how excited you were when you got your Xbox?"

"Yeah, I had been wanting one for a long time?"

"Why? Do you recall why you wanted one so badly?"

"Because they're cool, Grandma."

"Riiight...but I thought you told me that cool is an inside thing, that you're cool on the inside and nothing on the outside can make you cool. That's what you said when I told you broccoli would make you cool."

"Sure, but you can't play games online with your friends using broccoli. You need an Xbox for that."

"I see. So that's why you wanted an Xbox? To play games with your friends?"

"Yeah. Some of my friends live far away. My best friend, Henri, moved to Toronto. So every Tuesday and Friday night is game night."

"And when you play these games, do you talk to each other? Or do you just shoot down spaceships?

"We have headsets so we're talking to each other the whole time."

"I see. And do you just talk about the game, or do you talk about other things?"

"I don't know. We talk about a lot of stuff. I mean, we talk about the game we're playing, about strategy and stuff, but sometimes we talk about other junk. Henri's parents are going through a divorce, so we've been talking about that some. You know, it's kind of a tough time for him and his little sister."

Helena gave that air in which to circle above the table for a minute. Max had reached the apex of the conversation on his own without realizing it, so she would give it time to come in for a soft landing. Finally, she lit the runway to guide it in. "So the Xbox isn't about an Xbox at all, is it? It's about connection and relationship with Henri and your other friends; is that what you're saying?"

"Yeah, that's true. It's not about the machine; it's about spending time with my friends."

"And there you have it, Max. That's what makes life meaningful, isn't it? Wisdom is the awareness that life isn't about the things that make us feel good or give us comfort, it's about loving each other and being there for one another. It's not about the stuff we have or the things we know; it's about the love we share. Everything else is temporary. That phone you're holding, the Xbox you prize, even this time you're spending in the seventh grade—it all passes. The only thing that lasts is love. That's forever. The wise person sees this, believes this, and invests their whole life in this."

Max turned the phone back on himself, "There you have it, straight from the wisest woman I know. If you want meaning in your life, start by listening and end with loving. Nothing else will get you there."

Helena looked at the empty plate on Max's side of the table. "It looks like even cookies are temporary, Max."

2

The Conversation
We Need to Have
with Ourselves

MR. WEINENBERG SIGNED BOTH CONTRACTS WITH A BRILLIANTLY CRISP PEN. He punctuated the moment with a loud, ceremonial knuckle-crack before shaking my hand. He seemed genuinely pleased to be trying something new, an occurrence that clearly was a rarity. For my part, I felt like a young teenager whose first kiss was awkward, thrilling, and perplexing all at the same time. The emotions didn't live up to the hype. I was supposed to feel invigorated, validated, and self-satisfied, and when I returned to the office later there would be high fives and champaign. They would tell me this was a big deal, but I felt no different in that moment than when I had kicked the covers off while struggling to sleep twelve hours earlier. I was still just a lost kid trying to find my reason for being. Nothing had changed.

Walter Weinenberg ran a small, conservative, and financially strong bank, and he did it by doing things the exact same way for thirty years. This was 1988, but you wouldn't have known it by standing in his bank's lobby. The clacking sound of typewriters, not the clicking sound of computer keyboards, filled the air. The phones rang with bells rather than muted electronic tones. Bank tellers handwrote deposits and withdrawals into passbooks. To me, only a few years out of college, the whole scene smacked of 1958.

He walked me to the door, and we stepped into the August sunshine. Alone on the sidewalk, Mr. Weinenberg shook my hand again, but this time he held it as he put his other hand on my shoulder in a fatherlike way. "Let me tell you why I'm doing this," he said, with his eyes fixed on mine.

I was curious. The guy was notorious for never spending a nickel on advertising. This was only our third meeting, and I was walking out with a very significant contract for our AM radio station and a much larger one for our FM station. Something had gone right, but I had no idea what. "Please," I said. "The way you run your bank obviously works very well. You have an outstanding reputation, and you don't typically spend money on advertising. So why now?"

"I don't know why I agreed to meet with you the first time," he said. "I usually don't, but occasionally we all need to open ourselves up a bit, so on that day I guess I did. Anyway, do you remember the first thing you said to me?"

I shook my head. "Embarrassingly, no." I didn't even attempt to recall what I had said to him upon our first meeting. Instead, my mind was locked on his passing comment about how we all need to open ourselves up a bit sometimes. Those were wise words and I wanted to retain them.

"You asked about our customers. You didn't talk about your radio stations at all. I had to ask. You didn't brag about your ratings or your listeners. You just asked about our customers and why they choose to bank here. And do you remember what I said?"

"Of course," I said. That part I remembered. "It impressed me. You told me your customers are the most important people in the world, that they are mostly over fifty and worked hard their entire lives. You also said they bring their life savings to this bank with great faith that you'll help them ensure a secure retirement that's free from financial stress."

"Do you know you're the only sales rep who has ever come in here and asked about our customers? And I'm not just talking about TV and radio reps. I'm also talking about office supplies and technology." Mr. Weinenberg took a deep breath and shook his head. For the first time since I had met him, he looked human, vulnerable even. He spoke with a diction that was as exacting as his pen stroke. "I know we need to computerize our bank. We are behind the eight ball on that, but I am waiting for a computer systems salesperson to show up and convince me that he cares about the people we serve. Our customers deserve that from me. They deserve to be the number one priority in every decision I make, and that includes those with whom we do business."

Walter Weinenberg went on to explain how he went home that night and had a long conversation with his wife and his God. In his mid-fifties, he had been going through a crisis of meaning and purpose in his own life, questioning why he did what he did, why he battled with his board, and what meaningful difference it made. Our initial conversation had come at the right time for him, and it reignited his commitment to purpose. "There is a lot of stress around aging and finances in our culture," he said. "And frankly, a lot of big banks take advantage of that anxiety. They sell older people all sorts of products and services that are not really in their best interest."

A few members on the board of directors had been pressuring him to do the same, to accept as the bank's mission the responsibility to maximize profits for shareholders. This didn't quite sit right with Mr. Weinenberg. He, more than anybody, appreciated the need for financial strength and shareholder value, but he believed in the depth of his soul that those should be the result of good work not the reason for it.

"The board thinks we are in the money business. They are wrong," he told me during our second meeting. "We are in the stress management business. People need money to live, especially as they get older, and that causes a lot of stress. Even people with a lot of money stress over it. Sometimes they stress the most because they have the most to stress about. I have seen couples get divorced after forty years of marriage because they fought so much over money." He was on a roll, and his conviction was growing deeper as he progressed. "But they were not really fighting over money; they were fighting over anxiety. One of them was worried their money would run out, and they would end up in the poor house. Pretty soon the wife gets angry because he broke the lawnmower, or he gets ticked off because she went to lunch with friends and ordered dessert. It's crazy. Before you know it, they are afraid to breathe around each other. That's no way to live. My job is to help people live happily without all that nonsense."

Walter Weinenberg had discovered that his joy was derived from purpose, not from profits, and his purpose was to help people live securely and anxiety-free as they age. He believed he helped keep families intact and marriages together, and he had me convinced he was right. "People who are not stressed are much nicer to one another. Little things don't bother them. Stress comes from a dark place, and it's not from God," he told me. "It makes it hard for people to love each other."

I learned a lot about life from Mr. Weinenberg. I also learned a lot about myself, most notably that I felt far more fulfilled by inadvertently helping him reconnect with his purpose than I did by closing the deal and procuring lucrative commission checks. For me at the time, in my mid-twenties with college loans and a wife who was pregnant with our first child, that was a frightening realization. It was the first real lesson I learned about purpose and vocation—that it is going to scare the bejesus out of you. It is going to challenge you to choose between the inner voice of spirit whispering to your soul and the outer voice of culture promising false security. That is just how it is, and it is biblical. Moses, David, Nathanial, Mary, Jesus, Peter, Paul— all the great Bible heroes had to make this choice, and all chose to take the risk. No one wants to, of course. We'd all much prefer to play it safe.

In ten minutes of authentic disclosure, Walter Weinenberg taught me two more life-shaping lessons: first, the difference between a career and a vocation, and second, the single most important question we each need to ask ourselves. Before discussing those two things, I want to point out that Mr. Weinenberg was not nineteen years old. He was not a college sophomore staring into the mystery of a starry night while listening to Led Zeppelin and finding the meaning of life. He was in his fifties and had rounded the corner toward sixty. He was a banker complete with a starched shirt, cinched tie, and military compliant haircut. He had grandchildren, sat in the same pew every Sunday, and drove a Lincoln. This was not the sort of guy you would look at and sense he was lost, confused, seeking, or searching for his purpose. But, of course, he was. We all are. That's life.

We each need to have a serious conversation with ourselves about the relationship between career and purpose with an understanding that vocation is where they overlap, and I want to emphasize that this conversation continues well into retirement. Upon his much-anticipated retirement at sixty-seven, my friend Thom told everyone that his new career was golf. By the end of the first summer, Thom was as unhappy as he had ever been in all the years he was working. The second summer was even worse. And by the third summer he had become such a curmudgeon that no one wanted to golf with him. One day he got so upset over a poor round (when you have only one thing in your life it can too easily take on disproportional significance) that he gave his clubs away and canceled his country club membership. His wife couldn't stand to have him around the house, so he started volunteering at a local hospital, spending all day pushing people in wheelchairs, telling stories, laughing at jokes, and lifting spirits. Within days, he reported being much happier than he had ever been. And akin to Walter Weinenberg, he said, "I'm not in the wheelchair-pushing business; I'm in the spirit-lifting business." At the age of seventy, he found vocation and, with it, joy.

> We each need to have a serious conversation with ourselves about the relationship between career and purpose with an understanding that vocation is where they overlap.

Most of us start out by choosing a career, and when the excitement and newness wear off, we start hoping to squeeze some sense of meaning from the job, believing the next project or promotion will reignite our enthusiasm. We look to derive a sense of purpose from what we do rather than bring purpose to our work. In other words, we are seeking a backwards flow of vocation in which meaning flows back to us from our efforts, rather than flowing into the world through our efforts. Ultimately, it becomes a circular flow, but meaning and purpose must first find life within us and flow outwardly. That's worth repeating—purpose is something we must bring to our work long before it can ever become something we receive from our work.

Before venturing further, let's pause and sort out the relationship between career and vocation. These words get knotted up and entangled in ways that fuel confusion, often because the word "vocation" is ill-defined, and the word "career" is loaded with baggage. Additionally, vocation and career can happen in unison or entirely independently from one another. Simply stated, a career refers to what we do to put bread on our tables—teach school, build houses, sell insurance, drive trucks, etc. That's easy enough. From the time we're four years old, people want to talk to us about potential job interests, aptitudes, and development. What do you want to do when you grow up? We unintentionally plant seeds that start with what we might do rather than why we would do it. On one level, this makes sense. Career is concrete and kids can imagine being veterinarians and rock stars; purpose is esoteric. As a result, fourth graders who are barely turning ten years old will be exposed to career day at school, but when was the last time you heard of a school having vocation discernment day? It's not going to happen. More on that later, but here's a teaser: we start asking kids what they want to do long before they have any idea who they are.

For reasons that escape the constructs of my limited brain, my Catholic tradition speaks of *vocation* at street level almost exclusively in religio-sexual terms as a lifetime calling to live in either an ordained, avowed, married, or single state. While those are certainly aspects of vocations, they represent only one plane of a multidimensional life experience. Like a single side of a cube, they don't come close to telling the whole story. What happens if we open it up and think of *vocation* in spiritual terms, as the way we are each led to share our lives for the benefit of others? From this perspective, the idea of vocation moves beyond *what* we do, and expresses the heart, mind, and spirit with which we do it. Each morning as my son Jacob leaves for his clinic where he practices as a family physician, he says to his wife, "I'm going to help someone change their life today." That is the heart, mind, and spirit of purpose, and it is expressed through a vocation that he brings to his career.

Think of teachers, firefighters, nurses, coaches, and so many others who approach their work with the heart, mind, and spirit of purpose. Every day they touch the lives of others in very meaningful ways. My father, who worked as a carpenter, was laser-focused on the idea that he was creating and building environments that would inspire people to connect, communicate, and live in harmony with each other. His purpose was to inspire human unity, his career was carpentry, and his vocation was where they overlap. Even after he retired from his career, he continued to live with purpose and practice vocation; it just manifested differently. When he was in a rehab center at one point and had lost the ability to control speech, he would sit in a wheelchair outside his door and attempt to make eye contact and smile at everyone who walked past. His purpose was still to inspire human unity, his new vocation was to make eye contact and try to smile, and his "career" at the time was being a Parkinson's patient.

I find this understanding of purpose, vocation, and career to be useful because it respects the relationship while clarifying that two people can have the same career, but one can approach it as a vocation while the other does not. We all do things at various times in our lives, but we don't all do them with the same sense of purpose. Some people, as an example, approach parenthood as a vocation and others approach it merely as a function.

The concept of vocation I'm using refers to how each of us is called to use our gifts, time, and resources for the benefit of others individually or to serve humanity collectively. I'm fully aware that this is a more open definition than many are accustomed to, and it's likely that beads of sweat are forming on the palms of some Super Christians who are champing at the bit, waiting to shout, "Hold on, Heathen Steven! Where's God in this?! People who are called to a vocation are called to commit their lives in service to God!" Yup. No argument. Sure. Now tell me, who is *not* called to commit their lives in service to God? We all are, right? Who has *not* been given gifts to develop and share for the benefit of others? We're all called, and we've all been given gifts and resources to steward. Additionally, I'll throw Matthew 25:31–40 on the table: *whatsoever you do for the least, you do for me.* This is single-step logic: through our service to others, we serve God. For example, those who are called to parent a thirteen-year-old are definitely called to vocation, and it takes all of their heart, mind, and spirit to do so compassionately and mercifully. Don't even try to argue. I would also argue that those parents who approach parenting as a vocation and not merely as a chore or obligation will find it much more meaningful.

Under this construct, there are four dimensions of vocation:

1. The gifts, talents, resources, and time we've been given.
2. The personal disposition of our heart, mind, and spirit. This will drive our interests and passions.
3. The needs in the world that give us opportunity to serve others.
4. The socioeconomic structures that enable us to pursue the first three dimensions while caring for self and family. As part of my vocation as a father, I did have to consider my obligation to feed, house, and educate my children. Simultaneously, I had an obligation to nurture an awareness within my children that, as they ponder their own vocations, a just wage or salary is only one dimension and not the purpose of vocation.

My wife, Michelle, has a heart, mind, and spirit for peace and healing, and she has been given the gifts of a comforting presence and a gentle demeanor, so she has lived out her vocations as a social worker, a mother, a wife, and a healer. I have a heart, mind, and spirit for inspiring others to think deeply and understand things more profoundly, and I have been given the gifts of creative expression and synthesizing thought, enabling me to see the big picture and understand how relationships and dynamics work together. I have lived out my vocations as a writer, father, husband, and minister. Even in business, where I built a career helping companies build stronger, healthier relationships with customers and employees, I have done so by inspiring them to think deeply and understand things more profoundly. Through it all, an enriching and fulfilling sense of purpose has flowed through my work, but in all cases, it started as something I brought to the work, not as something I derived from the work.

Throughout our lives, we are called into an ongoing conversation with ourselves and our God about the first two dimensions of vocation—our gifts and our dispositions. At the heart of this conversation is an admission and an awareness that our gifts, talents, resources, and time are not really ours at all. They belong to our Creator, and we are trusted stewards of them. I cannot imagine a life of purpose and vocation that does not start with surrender to this reality. If you want to live a life that's deep in meaning, start with the admission that you came into this life with nothing and you'll leave with nothing, and then add in the realization that in between birth and death you still actually have nothing. Everything you think you have is actually on loan, and the minute you think you possess any of it, it possesses you. All any of us really have is an opportunity to love and serve others with compassion and joy, and God provides us with our own unique set of gifts and talents to do so.

Without this inner spiritual understanding, many of us are lured into the cultural mindset of self-interest and self-advancement. Like Jesus was in the desert, we are tempted to use our gifts and resources, along with our disposition of mind, heart, and spirit, to serve ego interests. From this perspective, some people want to become firefighters because it's a cool job, not because they have a disposition for service; some become teachers because they'll have summers off to travel, not because they have a disposition for education; and some become corporate attorneys because they want to amass personal wealth, not because they have a disposition for justice. It's worth emphasizing, however, that firefighters who bring a heart, mind, and spirit for service to their work still have cool jobs, teachers with a passion for education can still travel in the summer, and attorneys sincerely motivated by justice can still make a decent living. And in all cases, they're so much happier— not because they derive meaning from what they do, but because they bring meaning to everything they do. After all, if you have not cultivated meaning and purpose within you, you will never find it by looking outside of you.

3

The Conversation We Need to Have with Our Children

AT THE END OF MY NEPHEW'S CONFIRMATION CEREMONY, THE LOCAL BISHOP CALLED OUT THE NAMES OF TWELVE NEWLY CONFIRMED YOUNG MEN. He did so apparently randomly, drawing their names from a hat, and had each come to the front of the church. I imagined someone on the parish staff fielding this requirement form the chancery office, asking that the names of all the young men in the class be placed in a hat and presented to the bishop. Did this not strike anyone as odd? This is why I do not belong on a parish staff—I certainly would have filled the hat with fabricated names such as Karn Niverous and Chuck Thiseydea.

I wasn't sure how the young women felt about all this, if they felt excluded or relieved. Some seemed to express empathy for their male classmates, who shifted in their seats as though sitting on jagged rocks that had been baking in the hot sun. As each name was called, a collective breath was held, and a young man stood up like a tribute in *The Hunger Games*. They were each sixteen or seventeen years old, filled with all the confusion, anxieties, and social awkwardness of that life stage. Some were shy and reserved, some tried to look aloof and cool, and some sauntered with a false bravado. All were noticeably uncomfortable, sheep before the shearers. There, in front of their parents, grandparents, relatives, classmates, and the entire assembly, the bishop publicly asked each of these young men—whom he had never personally met—if they had thought about becoming a priest.

He didn't ask them about their gifts and talents. He didn't ask them about their hopes and dreams for the world. He didn't ask them about their struggles, stresses, and conflicts. He didn't even ask them their names. He simply moved from one young man to the next like a researcher doing an inventory of mice in a laboratory and, holding a microphone to the subject's face, he publicly asked if he had thought about becoming a priest.

"Holy cats!" I thought to myself. "This is how we're approaching the conversation about life's biggest questions: 'Why am I here? What is my purpose in life?' We just bypass the meaningful discernment questions and jump straight to public humiliation?"

When I was the age of these guys, I was lost and confused about so many things. I had no idea who I was. If my bishop had publicly asked me if I thought about becoming a priest, I would have very publicly lied. Right there, standing in church, immediately after being confirmed and receiving Holy Communion, I would have flat-out lied to my bishop just as surely as I would have lied to my dad about how fast I drove his car. I also would have lied if he asked me about becoming an actor or a writer or a mathematician. In truth, yes, the priesthood was on my mind, something I wondered if I was called to, but there was no way I would have stated so out loud in front of all my peers and family members. It was far too personal for me. It also would have labeled me at a time in my life when I wanted to dodge all labels. Not surprisingly, the answers these young men gave were mostly quipped dismissals: No, Bishop. Nope. No way. About five or six students in, a young man leaned into the microphone and said, "That would be a terrible idea."

Pausing, the bishop asked, "Why? God often calls the ones whom we least expect. Look at Saint Peter. He was a smelly fisherman who was rough around the edges, and he didn't catch on to things very fast. Yet he became our first pope."

This particular kid, though, was sharper than the bishop bargained. "Yes," he said. "But Saint Peter was married. He had a wife. And I like girls too much to become a priest." Yup, he went there. In church. What did the bishop expect, I wondered.

The bishop had a choice here. He could have smiled, shook the young man's hand, and kindly said, "Approach marriage as a vocation, ok? Bring love and life to others with great joy." Then he could have moved on. Or he could have laughed a little and said, "Yes, I understand. You have a lot of life ahead of you yet. I pray only that you bring an open heart and let the Holy Spirit guide you." And then he could have moved on. There are a hundred things he could have said, none of which should have been necessary because this whole scene was unnecessary, but all of which would have been better than the track he chose to drive this train down, which was to say, "I like girls, too. But we all have to give things up for God."

Oh, man, I thought to myself. How is he going to back out of this? Did he just denigrate the sacrament of marriage and suggest it doesn't involve sacrifice? And did he just refer to girls as *things to give up* like smoking or gambling? In fairness, this likely isn't what he meant. But the whole scene illustrates how counterproductive it is when we force this conversation on people, when we think we can push them or nudge them toward a vocation of our preference rather than inviting them to discern their vocation with the Spirit's guidance. It simply doesn't work, and it drives them further away. Also, it frames the conversation around *what* you do rather than *why* you do it, it prioritizes *vocation as career* over *vocation as an expression of purpose*, and it presumes a predetermined closed answer to what should be an open-ended question.

As the bishop neared the end of this lineup of young men whom he had assembled without their consent, he looked up at a clean-cut, snappy-looking guy in a dark jacket and tie who stood about six inches taller than he did. When the question was asked and the microphone was pushed north toward his face, this guy simply grabbed it, stepped forward, and spoke his truth confidently to the whole church: "With all due respect, Bishop, that question is the farthest thing from my mind right now. I am not ready for it." Wisdom. He didn't dismiss the question, he just recognized that he needed more years of growth and self-discovery before he would be prepared for it. I was proud of him and impressed by the people who raised him.

> The whole question around vocation applies to every single person, not just to those who are "churchy"; it is really a question about happiness and fulfillment in life...

The question about how a vocation manifests in anyone's life, at any point in life, should be a concluding question, not an opening salvo. It is where good discernment leads, not where it begins. When speaking with teens and young adults about their call to vocation, we have this tendency to start with a conclusion and then discern backward from that target, where the only answers are "yes," "no," and "I have no idea." All other possibilities are shelved until after this question is settled, leaving little room for the Holy Spirit to open new windows.

If we're going to have a spiritually informed conversation with ourselves and our children about how we're each called to live meaningfully, it would be wise to start in a much different place and give it a lot more time and space. We would be well advised to help our children understand that the whole question around vocation applies to every single person, not just to those who are "churchy"; that it is really a question about happiness and fulfillment in life; and that it is an open-ended spiritual question that pursues spiritual self-awareness, not a closed yes/no question about whether you're called to be a priest or a nun.

My wife and I raised three boys to adulthood. Somehow. It would be more accurate to say we helped God raise three boys to adulthood. In retrospect, I think we were mostly stagehands. From the get-go, we parented with a firm belief that these were God's children, created in God's own image and likeness, and that they each came prepackaged with everything needed to live meaningful and purposeful lives. This required having faith that God got it right when creating these kids, and that we should not try to re-form God's creative self-expressions in a way that was more to our liking. This can be very hard to remember when your five-year-old takes sidewalk chalk and draws all over the side of your freshly washed car, or when your thirteen-year-old tells you he hates you and wishes he had been born into a different family that doesn't have stupid rules regulating the intake of Mountain Dew.

From this perspective, we recognized that our job as parents was to give these kids rich soil and a healthy environment in which they could put down roots while growing toward the light. And that's it. We compared it to raising oak trees, not bonsai trees. In living out our vocation as parents, we were committed to providing the supporting nourishment for the boys to grow wholly into the person each was created to be. I share this because I believe the very first step in raising children on the road to a life filled with meaning and purpose is to understand the difference between raising them and shaping them. This is so critical because it sets a tone that lasts a lifetime, and it reframes the conversations we have with them and the dialog they have with themselves and with God.

For example, once our sons hit those all-important formative years starting around age twelve, we were very intentional about not asking them what they wanted to be or what they wanted to do when they grow up. They would each be asked those questions a hundred times by relatives, teachers, guidance counselors, and so many others. But those are rational, life-on-the-surface questions seeking rational, life-on-the-surface answers; the search for meaning and purpose is a spiritual pursuit seeking a spiritual path. You can't expect to see deeply while focusing on the surface, and you can't expect to discern a spiritual path by asking rational questions. One does not swim on the sidewalk. When asked, those questions anticipate answers, and Michelle and I felt it was our vocation as parents to encourage a path of discernment that encouraged pilgrimage and did not jump straight to destination.

When we think of the gospel passage about seeking and finding ("seek and you will find, knock and the door will be opened for you," Matthew 7:7), our emphasis is typically on the "finding" and the "door opening." We tend to gloss over the "seek" and the "knock" parts as though they are merely utilitarian instructions that need to be followed to reach the good stuff, like directions to point the cork away from your face when opening a bottle of champaign. But "seek" and "knock" are the verbs in Jesus' sentence, the action statements. They tell us not just what to do, but also how to live. Be a seeker! Be a knocker! The finding part will come in its own time, but only to those who live as seekers.

Looking around, I'm not convinced we in the West teach our children to be seekers and knockers. We place so much emphasis on test scores and grades, and we struggle to teach kids to fall in love with discovery and become lifelong pilgrims on a journey toward deeper understanding. In church, we teach them to follow rules but not how to ask questions. When one of my kids asked a religious education teacher why the Church excludes some people from Eucharist, I got an email telling me that my son was challenging the teaching and authority of the Church and was disruptive to the class. Think about that. Here we have a fourteen-year-old kid who is interested enough to show up and ask questions, and we shut him down because—why? Because his questions threaten the faith? If we're more interested in spoon-feeding answers than in wrestling with tough questions, what kind of a spirituality are we passing to the next generation? More to the point, how can we possibly expect kids to explore deep questions about purpose and vocation? We give our children a remarkable gift when we teach them to pry open questions and navigate the confusion and contradictions that follow. That's what most of life is all about; it's how we grow.

I recently read a social media post deriding children who don't accept "because I said so" as a reason for doing what is commanded by a parent or teacher. The insinuation was that kids who "don't know their place" and have the audacity to question authority are problematic in our society. Wow. I struggle to imagine something that disheartens the inspired curiosity of a child quite like being told their curiosity is disobedient. Yet how typical is this following exchange?

Parent: Turn off those video games
and go do your homework.
Child: I will in a minute.
Parent: Now, please.
Child: I just need to finish this level.
Parent: No, damnit! I said now!
Child: But...
Parent: But nothing! I'm the parent; now do as I say!
Child: But why can't I have a say in it? It's my life!
Parent: Because I said so!

There you have it. Do you see how quickly the conversation topic shifts from being about homework to being about authority? This conversation has played out almost verbatim in nearly every house where there is a parent and a twelve-year-old kid. The parent ends up frustrated, the kid ends up angry, and the relationship is strained. Love is diminished. And the kid's disposition toward education has been defined not as something they want to do or as an opportunity they get to pursue, but as a burden they must endure. Why? *Because I said so!*

Now imagine that same conversation going more like this:

Parent: How's your game going?

Child: Good. I'm just about done with this level.

Parent: Cool. When you're done, would you hit pause? I'll watch and wait.
(Short pause while parent has opportunity to sit with and observe their child.)

Child: OK, what?

Parent: First, I have a question about those spaceships you're flying.

Child: What?

Parent: How do you get them to jump into hyperdrive?

Child: It's easy. You just hold down "Y" and press the right paddle while pushing down on the joystick.

Parent: Sounds complicated. It must have taken a lot of programming.

Child: Yeah, I'm sure the code must be nuts to get graphics like that.

Parent: That's a lot of math and logic as well as a lot of graphics. Just look at the detail.

Child: I know, right? Each edition looks more real than the one before it.

Parent: Wouldn't it be cool to know how to write that code?

Child: Yeah, but if I was that smart, I don't think I'd waste it on video games.

Parent: Really? How would you use that gift?

Child: I'd work at finding a cure for cancer or something.

Parent: Did you know that a lot of surgeons train on video simulators? So do backhoe operators.

Child: So it's like a video game but instead of shooting aliens, you use lasers to blow up tumors?

Parent: Something like that. It's probably a good thing all those doctors, programmers, and graphic artists spent more time doing homework than playing video games.

Child: Seriously? That's what this is about?

Parent: What what's about?

Child: You went through this whole thing just to ask me if I did my homework?

Parent: No, I went through this whole thing because I wanted to have a conversation with you. Because I love you. You're important to me.

Child: Whatever.

Parent: But since you brought it up, how is your homework?

Child: It's almost done. I just have to go through some vocabulary words yet.

Parent: Why don't you go get them and I'll run through them with you?

Now, clearly, the second scenario takes way more effort and participation on the part of the parent. Many parents are exhausted and stressed out by the end of the day, with to-do lists that are three feet long and scant energy to get it all done. I get it. I've been there. When we get bogged down by the tasks of life—all the *whats* demanding to get done—we lose sight of the *why*. In the two dialog examples above, the first was focused on *what* needs to get done, and the second was focused on *why* we do it in the first place. This doesn't simply apply to the homework in the example, it applies to the act of parenting itself. In the second example, the parent clearly understands *why* they are a parent, and they do not let the *what* usurp that *why*. We struggle to see our role as parents, grandparents, aunts, uncles, teachers, and neighbors as vocational when we act from a *what*-based head rather than a *why*-based soul.

There are two things we all want in life that often get bulldozed when we merely manage our children rather than nurture them. First, we all want our lives to have meaning, and it is very difficult to come up with even a single thing that is as important and meaningful as raising these miraculous self-expressions of the Creator entrusted to our care. However, regardless of how meaningful something has the potential to be, we are required to invest ourselves in it before we experience it as meaningful. Again, meaning isn't something we get from life; it's something we bring to life. If we don't break ourselves open and pour ourselves into it, then life is just motion rather than meaning.

The second thing we all want is for our children to be happy, enriched, and fulfilled. We want them to embrace a life that's rich in purpose and meaning, because we know that's what leads to real happiness. This requires us, first, to role model such a life, and second, to nurture our kids on a path toward continuous wonder, growth, and discovery. The ongoing conversation we need to be having with our kids is one that looks for every opportunity to open them up rather than shut them down. Only then will they open themselves up to deep discernment about their own purpose and vocation in life.

Instead of asking preteens and teenagers career-based questions, we might consider looking for opportunities to engage in conversations around topics such as, what brings them joy? When do they feel most enriched and fulfilled? What's the most meaningful thing they did this week? What gifts and talents are they discovering in themselves? Who are their heroes, and what makes these people heroic in their eyes? Which other people have some of the same gifts they do, and how are they using those gifts to serve others or help humanity? (As an aside, these are worthwhile contemplative questions to be asking ourselves throughout our lives.)

The conversation we need to be having with (and role modeling for) our kids encourages them to look deeper, live deeper, listen deeper, and love deeper. This is how spiritual rootedness works and how it nourishes gifted, talented people created in God's own image to turn toward the light.

Along the way, there is great benefit to teaching our children the difference between rational and spiritual questions, and how to seek spiritual answers to the spiritual questions—how to listen with the heart, how to discern and not just think. Unless they learn to go deep and look within, they are apt to find the purpose of their own lives to be forever elusive. I've entered conversations with people ranging in age from seventeen all the way to their sixties and even seventies who are frustrated that God is not giving them a rational answer to the very spiritual question *what is the purpose of my life?* They keep looking for a grand sign outside of themselves, never realizing, as we've discussed earlier, that purpose and meaning are things we bring to life, not something we get from life.

4

Living as a Sower of Seeds

ALFRED MEYER, A DAIRY FARMER FROM LOYAL, WISCONSIN, WORE HIS TROUSERS ABOVE HIS GIRTH. He was stout by all accounts, somehow hiking his waistband over his roundness and cinching his belt about four inches below his armpits. As a twelve-year-old, I wondered where on earth he found such pants that measured the same from crotch to waistband as from crotch to cuff. But there he sat, this father of my father—the family member others said I most resembled—pontificating wisdom at the card table in my parents' living room.

When he got excited, his heavy lower lip quivered, and his thick fingers involuntarily rapped on the table with enough force to make the loose change bounce. And there was always loose change, mostly nickels and dimes stacked to the right of each player. We played Sheepshead. We always and only played Sheepshead with Grandpa. It was a religion complete with ritual and creed. And just as religion

is a vessel for spirituality, not a substitute for it, Sheepshead
with Grandpa Alfred was a vessel for conversation.

His lip was pulsing and his fingers were punctuating as
he spoke of world hunger and starvation on a Sunday after-
noon. If any issue bothered him more, I didn't know what
it was, and I didn't want to find out. "We are to feed the
hungry!" He underscored each of the last three words—
Feed The Hungry—with its own finger punch on the
tabletop. Forty-five cents bounced to the floor. "There is no
gosh damn reason people are starving to death anywhere
in this world! It's a sin! It's our biggest sin!" He was not a
man who used foul language lightly, at least not around his
grandchildren, so the very fact he let slip a "damn" further
alerted me to his intensity. "Farmers can produce plenty
of food to feed everyone, but the problem is distribution!
It's all politics! But you know what?" He pointed directly
at me as though furrowing a row in my soul and planting a
seed. "We can't just blame the politicians. Voters are just
as guilty. No one wants to talk about it! There are starving
children in this world, and no one wants to talk about it!
We'll talk about oil and inflation, but millions of children
are starving to death, and no one wants to talk about it!
We sit in church and pray about it all the time, but that's
where it stops. We want God to do all the work. When we
leave the church and go to the voting booth, no one cares
anymore." He wound it down a notch and spoke with sad-
ness. "We're only interested in those things that impact
our own lives, and we're not interested in the suffering of
other people. Show me one person," he was spinning up
again, "even one, who would give up a new car so some-

one else could feed their children." Seventy cents landed on the carpet.

As a farmer, Alfred Meyer approached his work and his social role with a strong sense of vocation. Deep at the very bottom of his heart, he believed beyond a sliver of doubt that his purpose in life was to feed the people of the world. This is what drove him forward, what got him out of bed in the morning. When the government announced agriculture programs to curb production, programs that would pay farmers to leave fields idle, he shook his head in frustration and bounced more nickels to the floor. He was greatly offended by the thought of cutting production while people on this planet were hungry. And the reality that many of his fellow farmers were lobbying in favor of these programs instead of lobbying for equitable global food distribution was almost more than he could handle.

I was very fortunate to have had grandparents and parents who role-modeled lives driven by meaning. They were not motivated by wealth, position, prestige, or power. Theirs was a value system I would have to grow older and deeper to appreciate. As a young teenager, I envied the lifestyles enjoyed by many of my classmates, and I quietly wished my lineage had been a little more wealth motivated. But my first and best teachers were not the sort of people who prioritized profit or privilege. Obviously, they wanted to earn a fair and just living to support their families, but they sought to do so while being driven by a sense of contribution. Work is meaningful, my father would teach me, not because of what we get from it, but because of how it enables us to contribute to the people, community, and world around us. I helped with the dishes, cleaned the garage, mowed the lawn, and swept out the basement not for payment, but because I was expected to contribute what I could as part of the family and a member of the household community. At the age of thirteen, I thought this was grossly unfair and accused my parents of exploiting child labor. But the seeds of contribution were sown in me, and decades later, I am profoundly grateful for all the enrichment and joy I've received from this life lesson— the primary purpose of our life's work is to contribute to a good greater than the self.

By the time I graduated university and entered the real world of work, I was astutely aware that my upbringing was more the exception than the rule. It was the mid-1980s, and the American dream had evolved from a chicken in every pot to a BMW in front of every McMansion. John F. Kennedy's inaugural instruction to "ask not what your country can do for you—ask what you can do for your country" had been replaced by Ronald Reagan's question, "Are you better off than you were four years ago?" From 1961 to 1981 the culture had moved from prioritizing contribution to prioritizing consumerism, and it showed in the dominant attitude toward work, vocation, marriage, and even friendships—*what's in it for me?*

Very early in my own career I was advised to be intentional and strategic about networking, which was code for choosing friends and building relationships with people who could help me advance my career. It struck me as disingenuous and smelled of objectifying people, seeing them not as expressions of the Creator but as resources to be tapped and used for personal advancement. Certainly, my lenses were tinted with naivete and idealism, and perhaps I was a little judgmental at that age, but the personal conflict I was having with the prevailing social order was authentic.

I had friends who shared my perspective, but we generally felt we were swimming against the current, as though approaching career as a vocation of service toward the greater good was the sort of thing done only by fringe idealists who listened to alternative music and wore shirts made of hemp. According to the unchallenged conventional wisdom of the time, the whole point of pursuing an education and developing a career was to put oneself in a position to build wealth and influence, eventually leading to that great golden ring called financial independence. This foundational premise was so culturally engrained that many people couldn't—and forty years later still can't— imagine any other reason for getting an education and going to work every day.

To clarify, I'm a huge fan of a fair wage and the dignity of independence. People should be justly compensated for their hard work and innovation. This is one of the pillars of Catholic social teaching, and it's not as though my parents raised me to eschew prosperity. The message they gave me was clear, however—financial gain should be an outcome of what you do, not the reason you do it. It's the result, not the purpose. My father was very intentional about this instruction, telling me on multiple occasions to never do anything for the money. I can still hear his voice as we sanded oak in his workshop, which for whatever reason always brought out his wisdom, "Never do anything for the money. Do it because you love it, and because it has value. If you do that, you'll never have to worry about money. The money will take care of itself."

I imagine a few readers are starting to get wound a bit sideways by all this. The hardcore capitalists who espouse Gordon Gekko's greed-is-good mantra will accuse me of being a socialist. Meanwhile, those on the other extreme of

> A simple and fair self-reflective question: Why do you do what you do? Why do you work? Why pursue education or other personal growth and development?

the ideological bell curve will accuse me of espousing a system that enables the exploitation of labor. To all of it, I have just one thing to say: Nonsense. I'm not talking about socioeconomic systems or theories here. I'm talking about internal motivation, a simple and fair self-reflective question: Why do you do what you do? Why do you work? Why pursue education or other personal growth and development?

Within many social and familial paradigms, personal growth and self-development are perceived to be wasted investments of time and money if they do not directly lead to a financial advantage. Again, this is conventionally accepted as sound logic, but rarely does anyone question its premise that *my life is exclusively for my own benefit*. If we dared to start with a different premise—that *my life is a gift I'm entrusted to steward for the greater good of God's people and creation*—the reasoning would be very different. It's no wonder so many people are burned out in their careers by the time they reach their early forties, that people hate their jobs and resent their employers. So many of us, alongside the people working next to us, are approaching our careers without a meaningful purpose and vocation beyond the boundaries of self. We've been taught to think in terms of personal rewards, and not in terms of personal contribution.

Obviously, there are some significant and noteworthy exceptions, with nurses, teachers, and ministers coming to mind among others. So many bright, energized, giving, and idealistic young people who pursue careers in education, health care, ministry, and social services burn out before middle age. Why is that? They enter these careers with a strong sense of purpose, intending to make a meaningful impact on the lives of others, but they end up feeling beaten up and beaten down. Instead of feeling socially validated and appreciated, they often feel misused and abused. They approach their work as contributors, but they are shackled within a context in which policy makers, administrators, patients, parents, and taxpayers objectify them. Grandpa Alfred was right—in a democracy, voters share responsibility for the formation of a culture and context driven by meaning and purpose. How we talk about that around our dinner tables has a profound effect on how our children discern and decide on their own careers.

I apologize for getting us sidetracked for a minute here. It's worth noting, however, that it would be too easy to point toward the people we know (and we all know a few) who burned out of careers driven by meaning and contribution, and then use that to dismiss the idea of pursuing such vocations. Again, these people seldom find that the work itself loses its purpose or value. Instead, they find that the systems and bureaucracies imposed on the work make it difficult, frustrating, and stressful.

As a farmer, Grandpa Alfred claimed he had little to do with the harvest. "That's God's business," he once told me. "God provides the sun and the rain. Heck, God even provides the fertilizer if you think about it. A farmer just spreads it." The farmer's primary job, he said, is to sow the seeds. "A good farmer is the one who focuses on putting seeds into healthy soil, not on how much he's going to store in his silos."

I don't know enough about the agricultural sciences to comment on whether that's a half-baked platitude or sage wisdom, but I've always taken it as good advice for life itself. Each of us is called to sow seeds of love, compassion, mercy, joy, and all good things without concern for the harvest. We don't know if or when our generosity and kindness will yield fruits, but we sow those seeds anyway. That's the difference between faith and investment. Those with faith are comfortable being contributors, leaving it to the Creator to supply whatever form of rain, sunshine, and fertilizer are needed to produce fruit. Harkening back to the earlier story of my father and his perspective on designing and building houses—he had no evidence that a family living in a house he built ultimately would connect and converse with each other in a healthy way, but he planted the seeds anyway. The same holds true for the front desk clerk welcoming travelers into a hotel, the middle school health teacher helping kids wrestle with their own well-being, the person stocking fresh produce on grocery shelves to feed families, the aspiring artist or poet hoping to open insights that lead people to awareness and compassion, and the seasoned accountant who is mentoring a protégé on ethics and wisdom. In most cases, living with meaning requires us to be content as sowers of seeds who might seldom see the harvest.

Simultaneously, if we are living with gratitude—a meaningful life is saturated with gratitude—we recognize that whatever harvest we reap results mostly from seeds others have planted. Character, I was told when I was still in my twenties, is shaped by the people we meet and the things we read. If this is true (and I suspect it mostly is), even the quality of our character is shaped and influenced by seeds others have planted. This recognition that all is gift, including each breath we take and every beat of our hearts, is a great defense against the self-important temptations of ego. Once freed from the prison of arrogance—that hall of deceptive mirrors tricking us into believing we are self-made and self-created—we are finally able to appreciate the value, meaning, and purpose of sowing seeds.

On a relatively routine basis, I encounter people who are steeped in midlife confusion about all this. They've done everything by the book, having raised their children with vocational diligence and sacred intention. For a lot of women, motherhood gave them purpose and, in many ways, defined their primary self-identity. Then, suddenly, their children have left home and are building lives of their own. These women look around and take stock of their own lives, realizing the world-changing dreams they had in their early twenties have evaporated in the pressure steam of parenting. Sometimes men who are fathers experience this as well, although it seems to afflict mothers more broadly and more deeply. In the words of one mother who seems to speak for a lot of women, "I'm in my fifties already, and what have I done? What have I achieved? I feel empty and a little adrift."

Such is the plight of the sower. We can spend the healthiest years of our lives raising families, giving our children rich soil that nourishes strong roots, but we don't necessarily get to see the fruits until a generation passes. What do you suppose Gandhi's mother said to herself? Or Jesus' mother? The fact that we don't directly see the harvest does not negate the value of sowing the seeds.

How healthy and helpful would it be if all parents and grandparents saw their role as my grandfather did when he looked straight at me while planting seeds of ethics and social responsibility, teaching me to think of a good greater than myself? When we sow the seeds of compassion, empathy, mercy, peace, kindness, and joy—these seeds of feed-the-hungry, give-drink-to-the-thirsty, care-for-the-sick—we may not reach the promised land in our lifetimes. We may not reap the harvest ourselves. But even Jesus had to die and rise before the seeds he had sown were able to blossom in full abundance. In all cases, though, a lifetime spent scattering these seeds without concern over whether they land on the footpath, rocky ground, or rich soil, will be fruitful, purposeful, and rich in meaning.

5

Finding Vocation in the River of Time

"YOU'RE LATE!" Cy Whitehawk barked, freezing my blood. There was no one I simultaneously admired and feared as much. With a mere sideways glance, Cy could intimidate the air into leaving the room.

"I'm so terribly sorry, Mr. Whitehawk. I mean no disrespect, but...." His hand went up and my throat went dry. I felt like a teenage boy facing his girlfriend's father after curfew. Cyrus Whitehawk had lived his entire life as the man I hoped to be but knew I would never become. There is a type of confidence earned only by winning a stare down with the devil himself; it's the only form of centered presence that leaves a wake, and Cy had it in such heft that it produced its own gravity. I was drawn toward him the same way thunderstorms draw me to the window, which is to say a one-to-one meeting with him was simultaneously awe-inspiring, marvelous, and terrifying, but also irresistible.

Stationed in the FBI's Chicago office throughout the 1970s and '80s, Cy made a career of going where angels fear to tread. He had danced toe to toe with drug lords and mob bosses, so I doubted there was anything about me he couldn't squash between his thumb and index finger without even looking up from his newspaper. Now in retirement, he had returned home to Keshena, Wisconsin, where he ran the Menominee Tribal Library. I doubted anyone failed to pay their late fees. Cy could have spent retirement on a golf course or at the beach; no one would have argued; he had earned it. "But why would I do that?" He told me during a previous meeting. "I can still do some good in the world." The way Cy framed it, he had moved to the Windy City years earlier to serve in the fight against crime, so retirement was time to come home and serve his people, "the people who gave me life, raised me with values, and made sure I was given a good education." Cy levered his entire life on a fulcrum of contribution, not consumerism, he gave without thought of receiving, and he sowed without concern for reaping. His operative question was *how can I serve the world?* Not *how can the world serve me?* I admired him for it.

As a young writer still in my mid-twenties, I lacked the good sense to realize a guy like Cy saw right through a kid like me. I wanted to impress him so badly, and that's exactly what I seemed to have done—impress him badly. At that point in my development, I wrote with the same motivation as magicians and illusionists, mostly flourishing about to distract people from noticing what was really going on. Because what was really going on was a mess.

I was a tadpole pretending to be a frog, a young, lost, and confused kid trying to convince the world (and perhaps mostly myself) that I was skilled at hopping and catching flies. Somehow, I had managed to win an assignment to write a few historical pieces for the Menominee Nation, which required access to archives at the tribal library. Thus the 9 a.m. appointment with Cy. But I was fifteen minutes late, an elephant I tried to obfuscate under a glittering blanket of feigned self-importance.

As I dashed into the small library that morning, my necktie and overcoat flew in behind me cartoonishly. Cy Whitehawk sat peacefully at a table facing the door. He wore the official uniform of a man who has nothing left to prove to anyone: blue jeans, a flannel shirt, and work boots. "You're late," he barked.

"I'm so terribly sorry, Mr. Whitehawk. I mean no disrespect, but I stopped into the office before driving out here, and you know how it is with messages and such," I stumbled and rambled like a hungover college student explaining to his professor why his term paper is late. "Anyway, three different people caught me on my way out the door, and by the time I got out of there it was 8:30 and I thought I would still make it on time, but there was farm traffic on the highway—I got stuck behind a tractor—and what should..."

"Stop," Cy took a deep breath and let the silence own the moment. I could hear a clock ticking in a nearby office, and all the air in the library became his again. He smiled and spoke with slow deliberation, "If you get this worked up over fifteen minutes, then you need to sit in silence for a bit and reconnect with the Great Spirit."

Was he telling me to shut up and pray? I tried to look stoic and appreciative, even though inside I was churning with vulnerability. My ruse was exposed, my soul laid bare. I reeked of insecurity poorly masked by a drug store cologne labeled *eau de self*, and he picked up my true scent even before the door closed behind me. Rather than put me at ease, he told me to shut up and pray. And to make matters worse, I knew he was right. It wasn't just good instruction in the moment; it was good advice for a lifetime.

"Here's what we're going to do," he spoke in a soft but authoritative voice. There would be no negotiation. "I'm going to finish reading this article. It'll take about ten minutes. While I do that, you'll just sit and breathe. When I'm done, we'll get coffee and hit the archives." He lowered his head and continued reading.

Slouching into the chair across from him, I reached for a *Time* magazine strewn among other periodicals on the wide oak table between us. As if by pure intuition or due to my transparent predictability, he slapped his bear-like hand on top of the exact issue I was reaching for and, without looking up, commanded very firmly, "Just. Sit."

I recoiled. And just sat, waiting, pondering, breathing, and mostly replaying his words mantra-like in my mind: *If you get this frazzled...sit in silence...reconnect with the Great Spirit.*

The adrenaline rush of a packed schedule was all I had known since high school. I was the antagonist in the Cat Steven's song "Father and Son," in which a man advises his presumably young adult son that life's happiness is found in slowing down, in pondering dreams and taking inventory of blessings, not in all the motion and commotion to which we easily get addicted. Many years later, when I was the father with adolescent sons, I would realize how spiritually immature the ambition of my younger self really was. I had tried to run away from my superficial self and run toward my imagined self, without realizing these were two versions of the same ego-driven illusion. Neither was real, and both were created in my own mind rather than in God's image. I wanted significance and importance, I wanted to matter, but my life's focus was on the noun "I" rather than the verb "contribute."

In fairness to my younger self, this is all part of growth. Each of us needs to bushwhack our own trail up the mountain of life that leads to spiritual awakening and, with it, true meaning. We're going to run mindlessly when we should walk mindfully, we're going to get knocked to our knees under the weight of the load, and we're going to trip and fall a few times. If you arrive at the summit of awareness without scrapes, cuts, and bruises, you likely climbed a very small hill and learned very little along the way.

One of the greatest barriers to living a life of meaning is the false notion that our purpose will come to us as a revelation rather than through journey and discovery. We'd prefer to take the trolly up the mountain, have a good dinner with slightly chilled wine, achieve full awareness of life's purpose as the sun sets, and then ride the trolly back down again in time to watch *The Bachelor* before falling asleep. But we can't be tourists in our own lives and expect to encounter meaning; we have to be pilgrims walking the path, getting dust in our throats and blisters on our feet. The quest for meaning, purpose, and vocation is not a comfortable pursuit.

> In reality, our purpose is an unfolding truth we discover throughout life's pilgrimage, a journey through which we encounter many unexpected twists and turns.

We spend much of life looking for easy answers and signs outside of ourselves, waiting for the clouds to part, the sky to open, and a beam of light to cast revelation upon us while a choir of angels sings a harmonious soundtrack. This certainly would be convenient, and we'd know with clear confidence what we are called to do. But that's simply not how it works for most of us. Even Jesus the Nazarene had to wander in the desert and face temptations before he was able to fully embrace his identity as Jesus the Christ. In the *Star Wars* universe, Luke Skywalker struggled and failed in the swamps while training under Master Yoda, and then he faced his own darkness in the caves of Dagobah before he understood that he was, indeed, the Jedi who could bring balance to the Force. From Ulysses in the *Odyssey* to Frodo Baggins in *Lord of the Rings*, the heroes in our timeless stories reveal an embedded human awareness that self-discovery demands a journey wrought with trials.

When examining the lives of the saints, we see this pattern again and again. Saint Francis and Saint John of the Cross are just two examples. Many of the great saints suffered through the pain of being lost for many years before they understood their true calling. Yet they tarried on in faith, wrestling with questions and confusion along the way. Meanwhile, we keep hoping the purpose of our lives will be revealed to us with little effort and no discomfort, thinking that perhaps a few days of relaxed and meditative peace while sitting in a cool mud bath at a resort spa will help us sort it out. Well, again, that's not how it works. Sorry.

In reality, our purpose is an unfolding truth we discover throughout life's pilgrimage, a journey through which we encounter many unexpected twists and turns. How in the world could you or I—how could anyone—truly discern meaning and purpose in a way that opens to vocation if we never wander with confusion through the desert, wrestle in the cold darkness with our own shadow side, climb the spiritual mountain, and finally collapse in parched exhaustion, fully emptied of ego? Only then can we finally get to know and love the authentic person God created each of us to be. That's when we're ready to start discovering purpose. But for any of that to happen, we have to step beyond the boundaries of our comfort zones—especially when our comfort zone is a spinning carrousel of busyness.

To summarize the point: 1) for most of us, meaning and purpose unfold throughout life's journey as we contemplatively wander ever deeper into mystery. We grow into them. Sometimes we might get flashes and glimpses for which we should be fully aware and grateful, but we shouldn't confuse the scent for the blossom. 2) A frantic pace that tries to leapfrog or short circuit the journey is counterproductive and is usually driven by ego rather than by spirit. You cannot find your center while you're dizzy. 3) The well-traveled journey will be wrought with stumbles, wrong turns, disappointments, and a sense of feeling lost. That's perfectly OK and expected. 4) Along the way, we must confront and wrestle with our shadow side. 5) The journey itself necessarily brings us into full encounter with our authentic self.

Bottom line—we grow into purpose and vocation over time, and it often evolves and changes throughout our life stages. We're so eager to ask kids still in high school what they want to do in life, and we train them for careers accordingly. But what do we do, really, to coach them on how to *sit in silence and reconnect with the Great Spirit?* Instead of giving adolescents and young adults permission to wander in the wilderness and encounter the person they were created to be, we expect them to lay the groundwork for a full speed assault on their life's work. We don't use those words per se, but the subtext is amplified in the cultural messages—load up on extracurricular involvement; play a sport or two or three; show leadership; challenge yourself with Advanced Placement courses; pile up service hours; get a job; be active in a church group; build your resumé. The message is overwhelmingly clear: run fast and furious toward a cultural image of success. It's a message built on the soft-sand fallacy that if you do more, you can become more. Here's an eye-opening question: What did Jesus do from age thirteen to thirty-three?

Instead of walking a path of formation and preparation, we end up water-bugging furiously across the surface of life until we reach our mid-forties or even later, never bothering to take a deep breath and look for the wisdom only found in a lifetime spent in the depths of quiet love.

In the midst of all this, natural introverts and others who tend to be deep thinkers are at risk of feeling overwhelmed, or worse yet, somehow socially broken. Our familial and social systems do not teach and value true introspection. The combined volume of social and cultural voices overpowers the stirring whispers deep within. Yet within this context we expect people to consider purpose and vocation. Is it any wonder that we're all racing feverishly into the abyss of middle age before exploring the meaning and purpose of it all?

Has it occurred to us that the underlying message we end up showering upon our youth during their most formative years is that who they are is not enough? In claiming to want what's best (whatever that foggy notion means) for our children, we haven't really explored what we mean by *best*. In a conversation about my own vocational discernment in my mid-thirties, I mentioned to one of my mentors, Fr. Jim Dillenberg, that "I want to make sure I live up to my full potential."

He wisely looked at me and said, "I hear people say that all the time, but I don't know what it means. If you love God and you love your neighbor, isn't that your full potential? What else is there?"

In that moment, I realized that this notion of *best* had been baked into me since middle school. I used the language and assumed it to be true even though I had never thought about what it means. How in heaven or on earth could I ever hope to live a life filled with meaning when I was operating on some sort of programmed autopilot?

Unless we go through the spiritual discernment process of determining what purpose and vocation mean for us individually, we are at risk of pursuing it comparatively. Indeed, part of our social programming is to compete against others, not just in sport but in character, quality, and overall achievement, sometimes even in morality. (Yes, there is competitive morality in which grown adults subtly maneuver to out-Christian others. It's sad.) High performers too easily develop a false sense of superiority, while others develop a false sense of inferiority. The developmental focus is on who we think we ought to become in order to succeed in society rather than who we are created to be as an expression of God's likeness.

The pursuit of a life filled with meaning and purpose is built on the bedrock of this relatively straightforward question: *How am I called to reveal God's image and likeness to the world?* Helpful hint here: God's image and likeness is love. And authentic love is never comparative or competitive. It's simply given away generously and radically with abundance and abandon. Sadly, the question, "How am I called to reveal God's love in the world?" (something we can all do everywhere all the time) is seldom even on the radar when we search for purpose and meaning. We think it is the output rather than the input, the finish line rather than the starting line.

Even the religious instruction we provide typically focuses on the outward, external expression and behavior of the person. Seldom does it introduce internal discernment and true spiritual encounter. A life of wholeness requires us to nurture the sacred within and then express it lovingly into our relationships and community, while also opening our awareness to the awe-inspiring sacredness of the people and creation around us. In other words, give and receive love in an endless cycle of unity with all creation. This is where we find meaning, purpose, and vocation.

As a kid, the only time I was invited to sit in silence was as a punishment for misbehaving. The words varied, but the theme was consistent: *Go stand in the corner. Go to your room. Put your head down on your desk. I don't want to hear another word out of you. Sit there and think about what you've done.* We were hardworking stock who valued productivity, so sitting in quiet silence was not presented as a noble pursuit, and it's certainly not how the nuns taught us to pray. My father and my grandfathers, however, could spend entire days in silence as they went about their work. After all, a man on a tractor with no radio has an opportunity to spend a lot of time with God. As I watched my father go about his work sanding, assembling, and finishing cabinets, I observed his patience and reverence. His work was prayerful and contemplative. A real vocation, I eventually grew to realize, is one in which the work is done with prayerful reverence, and this can apply to just about anyone doing anything from tending a garden to removing a brain tumor. But first, we have to allow ourselves to be awed, which also means being humbled.

If you want to live a meaningful life, approach everything you do and everyone you meet with prayerful reverence, recognizing, as mentioned earlier, that meaning is something we bring to life, not something we always get from life.

Cy Whitehawk looked at me, a white kid in his twenties who was at risk of becoming roadkill on the proverbial fast track, and he recognized that I was splattered across life's surface. By saying *if you get this frazzled...sit in silence... reconnect with the Great Spirit,* he reframed the benefit of introspection. When we find ourselves all angst up over the time spent delayed in traffic or waiting in line, what self-talk is taking place in our heads? Are we more apt to say, "C'mon, hurry up! I don't have time for this. Let's go people!" or will we say, "Wow, if I have this much anxiety over a few minutes, I need to take a deep breath and reconnect with God." The first option leads us along a winding path of meaningless movement that goes nowhere; the second leads us into a deeper encounter with meaning and purpose.

While digging through the tribal archives, I realized there exists no record of how long the Menominee people have lived along the Wolf River in North-Central Wisconsin. No one knows. One article suggested tribal ancestors have been on that land for at least eight thousand years. Whether that's true or not, their presence predates their written history by thousands of years. Perhaps if I had roots deeper than my own age, I would have had a different perspective on fifteen minutes.

Many Native American cultures guide their decision making with a seven generations perspective. By acknowledging that they stand in a river of time, they express gratitude for previous generations who have affected their current experience, and they feel an obligation to positively affect the lives of future generations. Embracing this mindset will expand our thinking about the meaning and purpose of our own lives.

The purpose of my own life may be paving the way for possibilities that will manifest long after I'm gone. Earlier I wrote about my father and my grandfather, who both passed away before I published my first book. Yet their influence, guidance, and example had a profound effect on me. Their lives, along with the lives of my mother, grandmothers, teachers, authors, artists, and many others, including Cy Whitehawk, have contributed great insight to the words you are now reading. Think about this. By intertwining the meaning of my life with the lives of others who have gone before me and will come after me, I disempower the ego-narrative of the self-made man. It is exposed as fraudulent and shortsighted. Instead, I open myself to a purpose and vocation that lives long after me and way beyond me. It liberates me from the self-imposed pressure to do great things, and it invites me to simply love others abundantly and share myself generously.

After all, what could be more meaningful than that?

6

Gifts Discernment as a Way of Life

MICHELLE SMILED. If our roles had been reversed, I doubt I would have been so centered and present. But there she stood, waiting by baggage claim, like filtered sunlight after a summer storm. She wore a soft white t-shirt with a taupe skirt and sandals. A small gold pendent in the shape of a scallop shell—the symbol of a pilgrim on the road to Santiago de Compostela—hung from a thin chain around her neck. In a world of plastics and metals, she was earth, the original clay into which the Creator blew the first breaths of life. It was no wonder she often felt out of place among the social synthetics of small talk and banal chatter. For my money, she was the one person I knew who was unabashedly in place, rooted and grounded. I was blessed that my roots had become entangled with hers. Her grip on reality was strong enough to keep me planted as well.

It was late, a few minutes past ten, nearly five hours later than my plane had been scheduled to arrive. Had things gone as planned, I would have been home for dinner with the family, home to help with dishes, and home to tell a bed-time story to Adam who, at the age of five, much preferred the stories I made up to stories read from books. After four days of travel and meetings culminating in weather delays, I was zombie-like. My thoughts were turned inward, self-ishly focused on my own weariness, as they typically are when people feel depleted. I sincerely appreciated that Michelle had come to pick me up, but I hadn't fully con-sidered what a great inconvenience this was for her. She was a morning person, often beating the sunrise to dawn, which also meant that she normally retired for the evening by half past eight. As a part-time social worker and a full-time mother, most of her life was spent anticipating and responding to the needs of others. Here she was again, extending her day in response to my needs, and I was too self-absorbed to be humbled by it.

As we waited for my bag to come down the chute, we exchanged all the catch-up inquiries mandatory for the situation. How are the kids? How was your flight? How was Alex's soccer game? Did your meetings go well? What would you like to do this weekend? They were mostly innocuous questions that were easy to ask and required the other person to do most of the thinking.

Across the way, a mid-fifties-ish man with mid-fifties-ish dimensions had been watching us. At first it seemed coincidental, but it continued long enough to be obviously intentional. He wasn't watching people; he was watching us. I pretended not to notice, but it finally reached a point where brief eye contact was inevitable. I tried to place him but couldn't. He wore khaki golf slacks and a light blue button-down shirt with an open collar, like nearly every other middle-aged traveler I had seen in airports throughout the day. He grabbed his bag from the conveyor and weaved through the throng toward us. My brain raced. How did he know me? What was his name? I braced myself for the inevitable awkwardness that occurs when you're greeted with familiarity by someone you do not recognize and cannot place.

When he reached us, he looked right past me and shook Michelle's hand. "Y'alls Michelle, right?" he asked, sounding like he had a pinch of snuff in his cheek. "We met in person just once but spoke many times on the phone. I'm Bobby Winsczecki. You took care of my momma." Part of me was relieved that he and I had not met previously; it was not a brain lapse on my part. And part of me was embarrassed that I had assumed he had recognized me, and it hadn't occurred to me that he had recognized Michelle.

"Yes, of course, Mr. Winsczecki. Your mother was such a wonderful person. She had a gentle way about her. I'm so sorry for your loss." Michelle held his hand as she spoke, erasing any distance between them. I was impressed by her presence and poise, along with her very generous and empathetic kindness. It was late. She was tired, and she had already spent her entire day in service to others. If she resented being asked to play the social worker after 10 p.m. at airport baggage claim, it didn't show at all. She was the embodiment of grace, an existential contrast to who I was in that same time and space. Her centering purpose was outward-focused in service to others; mine was inward-focused, mostly concerned with the comfort of self.

I needn't tell you whose life was happier and more meaningful in that moment.

Bobby Winsczecki turned and introduced himself to me, but before I could get my name out, he spilled his story and Michelle's role in it. "I live in Texas and my momma was dyin' in the care facility up here where your wife works. Alzheimer's. It was a tough road. I got no siblings, so it's just me, and I tried to get up here to Wisconsin as often as I could, but Michelle was my only link through it all. I don't think I ever woulda gotten through this without her kindness. I really don't. She was my angel when I needed it most. God bless her. She helped me so much — not just with the logistics of momma's care during the final days and the funeral planning and all that, but with my own emotions."

I was deeply moved by his shared authenticity and gratitude, while also being both impressed and inspired by my wife. Her work, I realized in the moment, was so much more valuable than my own. I was working as a creative director and strategist for an advertising agency, and I realized in that moment how board rooms, titles, and pay stubs conspire to create an illusion of importance and value. It's a golden calf, really. Arguably, idolatry. We too easily dupe ourselves into thinking the value of our work is somehow linked to the compensation, social prestige, and other trophies. It's a ruse, a dangerous ruse, luring us into the false notion that the fruits of our labors are tallied in our position and compensation. By this measure, the image of Christ crucified represents utter failure rather than total victory. Standing in the airport, weary and exhausted, it quickly and abundantly became clear to me that there is only one true measure of the value of one's work: how effectively it lifts the lives of others.

This does not in any way devalue the work of those with gifts for business, manufacturing, or other pursuits, nor does it elevate the work of teachers, social workers, ministers, and the like. We've all met plenty of people in business, service positions, and skilled trades who are very focused on lifting others and having a positive impact on the world around them, and we've all met educators, health care workers, and ministers who lack compassion and are mostly self-serving. Again, the difference isn't *what* you do, it's *why* you do it. The greater good needs people in all walks of life who work with honesty, integrity, and a sincere desire to contribute their time and talent to the well-being of other people. This is true of everyone from electricians, street sweepers, and auto mechanics to childcare workers, middle school aids, and county clerks. As Grandpa Alfred once explained it, "Two farmers each hooked a spreader to their tractors and headed out to the field. One thought he was helping God produce food to feed the world; the other figured he was just spreading manure. Who do you think went to bed happier at the end of the day?"

One more time: it's not *what* you do; it's *why* you do it. And meaning isn't something we get out of life; it's something we bring to life.

Driving home through the dark streets that night, I looked over at Michelle's profile illuminated by the dashboard lights. I saw her differently and with a tinge of respectful envy. As a mother, she broke herself open and poured herself out for our children. They, their development, and their well-being came first, and she held me to that same standard as a father. I was coming home to children who were almost always bursting with laughter, discovery, imagination, music, and creativity. There were certainly conflicts, arguments, and mood swings, but nearly every day and every dinner were ripe with loving joy. The gifts she tilled into the fertile soil of family are not measured or scored by talent assessment tools. We don't think of fostering healthy environments, nurturing a love for learning, and encouraging imaginative play as talents. But they are! Michelle brought these same vocational gifts, although expressed and manifest differently, into her work as a geriatric social worker. She seemed to have one consistent measure of success—how effectively and compassionately she touched the lives of others, lifted them up, and alleviated suffering. That's meaningful, purposeful, and vocational.

With three children and a mortgage, I did not have the luxury of switching careers to find meaning and purpose, but I realized I didn't need to. I simply needed to shift my focus away from how my career was impacting me and my life and focus instead on how I was impacting the lives of others. I needed to shift my head and heart toward feeding people and away from spreading manure. Looking around at the people with whom I worked, I saw their humanity, vulnerability, hopes, and dreams. I realized how much I genuinely loved them, and I became determined to help foster an environment in which they could find real value and meaning in their work. Instead of chasing money,

I chased meaning by developing relationships with clients who were mission-driven and doing positive things to impact humanity. These included health care organizations, a fire truck manufacturer, credit unions, and others who were faithful to a mission that served a good greater than self. While some of these were not-for-profit organizations, many were for-profit, but they regarded profit as the result of their work, not the purpose for their work. When searching for meaning and purpose in life, motivation matters. Regardless of what we are doing, we will never find deep meaning if our motivation is superficial.

The inside-out shift in my focus—from how I was benefitting from my work to how my work could raise up other people—required a renewed talent evaluation on my part. For the first time, I saw servant leadership as a talent, not merely as a strategic disposition. Likewise, I grew to realize that developing a collaborative and supportive work culture, holding a steady keel amid stormy turbulence, and keeping a ship pointed at a north star are all talents, and developing these gifts within myself was not about personal career advancement; it was about providing an opportunity for people to come to work each day, collaborate with others to put something good in the world, and support their families in the process. We often categorize these gifts as leadership skills, but I've grown to see them as more than skills; they are gifts and talents. While, like tennis, they can be taught and practiced, some people have a more natural predilection for them.

Michelle is indeed tremendously gifted and talented in ways I can see but can never reach. Certainly, I can learn some listening skills and practice attentive presence, but I could no more achieve her level than I could become a world-class pianist. She has a gift, a very calming presence about her, an energy in which others feel comfortable and safe. When she enters a room, peace comes with her. It's such a valuable and vital gift, but one we typically do not even recognize.

When doing talent discernment with high school students or anyone else for that matter, no one identifies the seeds of these types of gifts, nor do we talk about the Bobby Winsczecki airport moments and the way we impact the lives of others. Even when they are acknowledged, they are easily recast as "soft skills" and considered supplemental rather than core talents. Why? When I look at them through the lens of my Christian faith tradition, these are the types of gifts Jesus most often role modeled. The gospels don't even mention his talent for carpentry, his mastery of culinary arts, or his brilliance as a naturalist, but they talk a lot about his ability to connect with people in a way that opened their hearts to love and to healing. These are the

> When searching for meaning and purpose in life, motivation matters. Regardless of what we are doing, we will never find deep meaning if our motivation is superficial.

gifts that often cultivate slowly over a lifetime of experience. They are typically underdeveloped in the spiritual immaturity of our youth, only emerging later like autumn flowers. Slowly, gradually, they germinate and grow under the surface, coming to fruition only after years of spiritual growth and ongoing personal development.

Gifts discernment is too often reduced to a ninety-minute exercise we do with kids in high school, with outputs tending to focus more on what the person is good at rather than how they project God's image in the world. If someone is "good at" algebra, we say they have a gift for math. Likewise, if they are "good at" athletics, music, art, science, technology, and so forth. Basically, we tend to identify talents based on objective comparatives rather than innate characteristics. We look through a functional lens, which entices us to jump right to the *what*—what you can do better than others in a way that has market value, bypassing any discernment about the unique image of God each person is created to reveal, or where that person finds meaning and purpose.

Baked into this stew is the false and unfortunate notion that our gifts are hardwired into us and must be exceptional to qualify as talent. We evaluate based on the fruits rather than the seeds. Kids as young as nine years old who do not bring home rocket scores on math quizzes assume they don't have a gift for math, and they believe that will never change. We create an imprint on the mind and even in the heart that thinks of talent as programmed like DNA.

Human development is ongoing and doesn't stop when we reach the age of twenty-one or twenty-five. Intellectual, emotional, and spiritual growth continue throughout our life. Many meaningful and high-value talents take half a lifetime or more to emerge, and we discover them when we're in our forties, fifties, or even later. And as new gifts emerge, our purpose may also evolve. If you think about it, this is a big part of what makes life's journey so rich and rewarding. We keep discovering new things about ourselves and about one another.

When I was a child, my mother was rather introverted, a balance to my father's very social, confident, and extroverted nature. Large crowds and gatherings drained her energy. And while she was very responsive to social obligations, and she certainly valued and respected people, she would have been very happy to stay home and sit at her sewing machine if my dad didn't "drag her places," as she put it. When my father passed away, there was every reason to be concerned she would be socially isolated and even reclusive. But in the months and years that followed, even under the weight of her deep grief, she developed this profound gift for connecting with people. Looking around the condominium building where she lived, she noticed many other people who were widowed and living alone. She found it within herself to reach out. Soon she began delivering cookies or dropping by with books and wine.

During my father's progressive illness, my mom found purpose in her role as primary caregiver. This gave her meaning and vocation she hadn't anticipated or planned earlier in her life. After my dad's death, she found another unexpected purpose, and with it a vocation (one might argue the vocation found her, as vocations often do). She discovered and shared a gift for fostering relationship, community, and a valuable sense of inclusion and belonging. It's worth noting that she brought forth this sense of contribution—and with it purpose and meaning—from within herself. It took effort, and if she had focused on the *what* rather than on the *why*, there is a good chance she would not have found the energy.

If we restrict gifts discernment only to our developmental years, we inadvertently consider vocation exclusively in the context of career choice. In doing so, we greatly risk shortchanging much of life's journey. A young tree brings the gift of delight and newness. A maturing tree brings the gift of spring blossoms and late summer fruits. A mature tree brings the gift of generous shade. As we progress along life's journey, the gifts we share emerge, overlap, and evolve.

A robust and healthy spirituality continuously calls us to live in the moment, to be present with an abiding awareness that each day is a new creation. In that, we are invited into gifts discernment anew with each rotation of the earth on its axis and each revolution around the sun. If we are truly living a pilgrim's journey through this life, we will be growing and discovering with each footfall upon the path, opening to a realization that the daily bread we are gifted at each new dawn nourishes us with a deeper awareness of purpose, new opportunities to lovingly deliver on that purpose, and the gifts we need to do so effectively.

But none of this happens to us; it happens through us. The person who is consistently delighted by the miracles of life, laughter, and love is the one who lives in an awareness of ongoing revelation. A practice of daily gifts discernment awakens us to the unfolding truth of a deeper reality. Even if I don't discover new gifts on this day, I will discover new opportunities to share my gifts in meaningful ways.

7

Living Inside-Out: Vocation Follows Identity

JOHN IS NINETY YEARS OLD. His energy has waned, and he claims his memory has declined some, but it seems every bit as sharp as mine, which may be why he thinks it has been compromised. Fair enough. He reads a lot of everything, thinks deeply, has a real gift for engaging, meaningful conversation, and has not yet grown cynical or given up on humanity. Age may have taken him away from the motorcycle he used to ride through the Belgian countryside, but it has ripened his humor and seasoned his compassion. Besides, the Belgian countryside now rides through him. For my money, that's what wisdom looks like.

In the current iteration of his vocation, he has become the primary care companion to Monique-Thérèse, a woman who lives in the memory unit of a long-term care facility. Recently, he started saying Sunday Mass for the residents in that community. You see, John is Fr. John, a retired Catholic priest or, more accurately, a senior priest, since priests, like parents, don't ever really retire, try as they may. He prefers to be called John, rather than Fr. John, because he prefers mutuality in his relationships, and while the priesthood may have been his vocation, it is not his identity.

I wonder how often our search for purpose and vocation is really a search for identity and significance. We look for a role or an impact outside of ourselves, like we did as teens when we hoped that being a star athlete or a straight-A student would define us and give us significance, but then we graduated from high school and realized none of it really mattered. Still, though, we were socially conditioned to think we'll have value and importance when others acknowledge us as valuable and important. We substitute varsity letters and honor roll accolades with job titles, academic degrees, bigger homes, and uniforms that express an outward image we believe others will respect and even admire. None of it, though, speaks to who we are in our heart and soul. It is all a façade. Our only authentic identity is, of course, inherent in our sacred nature as a living, breathing expression of our Creator's own image. We cannot derive identity from vocation; instead, we derive vocation from purpose, and purpose from our identity. We must do the deep spiritual work of discovering and embracing who we authentically are as an expression of our Creator before we discover true meaning.

Over the years, I've listened to people confess to having become priests, mothers, social workers, doctors, police officers, truck drivers, bankers, professors, soldiers, and a whole bunch of other things because they were hoping it would give them an identity with respect and value. In some cases, they had hoped it would make them more lovable within their family systems. Usually by the time they're in their mid-forties, they realize this was a failed strategy, but by then they're stuck in a career that was never actually a calling or vocation. What we think of as a midlife crisis just might be a midlife awakening.

The sequence is backwards. Vocation follows identity, not the other way around. The point is worth restating: we don't get our identity from position or title; we get it from our sacred creation in God's image. When we hope to gain identity from vocation rather than seeking vocation from identity, both remain elusive. Living with meaning and purpose requires us to reverse the flow and live from the inside-out, a process I've come to think of as spiritually growing up. It can take a lifetime, and that's OK.

To even the score for whatever rubrics he compromised or vespers he abridged, John has been given the penance of my enduring friendship. Five spins on a rosary while kneeling on Legos would have been more just and required less patience. In exchange for a shared bottle of wine every few weeks, he provides me with wisdom, spiritual guidance, insight, encouragement, kindness, and a solution to all the world's problems. In John's mind, that solution is universal and uncomplicated—love one another, which seems ironically rare and complex.

Among the many profound insights into joy that John has given me is the spiritual value of living inside-out rather than outside-in. He has never actually used those words, nor would he have needed to; he speaks with his actions and disposition. It's his chosen way of life, an authentic expression of his identity. Most of us spend our days on earth with life's energy flowing in the reverse direction. We live in response to stimuli, with our thoughts and emotions responding to the experience and validation we are receiving (or not receiving) from the people and events around us.

As a relatively benign example, think of a time you wanted to check out at a convenience store and had to wait a bit because the cashier was on his phone. We've all been there. If you're like me (and may God help you if you are), you probably got annoyed and maybe even a bit cheesed. After all, the clerk's failure to see you as the most important person in his world right then and there was flat out rude. Right? It's his job for crying out loud! While we stand there steaming with clenched jaws and rolling eyes, it doesn't occur to us that he might be checking on his elderly grandparent or awaiting news on his brother's biopsy. Or he might be checking on a sick child or reading an email from his military recruiter or responding to a text from his boss asking him to work late. Frankly, we don't even acknowledge his humanity; we objectify him as a resource whose purpose is to meet our immediate need, so we don't think about why he's on his phone, nor do we care. We're just upset that he is not recognizing us as his single greatest priority, causing us to wait a moment. During those seconds in our lives, we often surrender our mood to the pettiness of an offended ego. Instead of letting joy flow through us into the world, we are consumed by annoyance and frustration. What's more—

> People who live like they mean it always realize they have a choice, and they choose to put peace, joy, kindness, hope, mercy, and love in the world regardless of what the world is giving them in the moment.

it just happens. We don't even pause to realize we have a choice.

John's example has taught me that people who live like they mean it always realize they have a choice, and they choose to put peace, joy, kindness, hope, mercy, and love in the world regardless of what the world is giving them in the moment. This is a Jesus-on-the-cross approach to life, and it's inside-out. Ultimately, it all comes full circle in the end—we experience what we create, but a good life is a creation initiative, not an investment strategy. People who are living with a deep sense of meaning and purpose share joy purely to share joy. They foster kindness purely to foster kindness. And they live with compassion purely to live with compassion. They do it because the world needs it and they're able to provide it, not because they hope to be rewarded for it here on earth or in a future heaven.

I got to witness this in live action as I was driving with a colleague, Chris. He received a call from the automobile repair shop—where his car had been for two weeks—letting him know that the part they were waiting for had finally arrived, but not really. It was the wrong part. He would be without his car for at least two more weeks. I only heard his side of the conversation, but it went like this: "Hi, this is Chris....oh, hi, Sara, how's your Tuesday?...It's really good, thanks for asking....Uh-oh...I see....Well, dang, that's gotta be frustrating for you....So it's going to be at least two more weeks?...OK, well, worse tragedies have befallen humanity....No, thanks for asking, though. I can manage until then. Hey, listen Sara, I really appreciate you guys working on this. I really do. I'm sorry it has become a bit of a logistical hairball for you....No worries at all. Just let me know when it comes together. Thank you for calling. Have a great day, Sara! Bye."

Let's reset that for a moment. Chris had been without his car for two weeks, a significant inconvenience for him. He was anxious to get it back, as most of us would be. The repair shop was telling him that instead of having it fixed, it was going to be at least another two weeks because someone messed up. And Chris' response was to express gratitude and empathize with the repair shop. Some might think Chris was being a pushover, allowing the repair shop to walk all over him. But that's not how he saw it at all. He was in complete control of his own life experience, and he was choosing to deal with adversity in a way that was positive rather than negative, a way that was supportive rather than confrontational.

When he got off the phone, Hoda, a third person in the car with us, wanted to understand more about Chris' response.

Hoda: Are you always like that on the phone?
You are, aren't you?

Chris: Like what?

Hoda: Like making the other person feel better
about delivering bad news.

Chris: Well, it's not her fault someone sent the
wrong part.

Hoda: What if she's covering her tracks?
What if she ordered the wrong part?

Chris: That's an assumptive and cynical way of
looking at things, but even if that's the case,
it was an innocent mistake. It happens.

Hoda: But are you always like that? Are you always
helping people feel better about stuff?

Chris: I don't know. I hope so. It's my goal that
everyone leaves a conversation with me feeling
a bit uplifted, like life is just a notch brighter.

Hoda: But aren't you upset about your car?

Chris: Sure, it's a bit frustrating, but I could spend
most of my life being upset about something
if I think that way. Life's too short. I'd rather
think about how I'm treating the world than
worry about how the world is treating me.

Chris lived like he meant it. As a result, peace and joy seemed to enter every room with him. Even when navigating the difficult trials of life that we all face, he held his keel. Storm waves crashed across his bow just like everyone else's, but they did not seem to rock his boat.

Choosing to live in the other direction—worrying more about how the world and its inhabitants are affecting us— becomes a tamed-down version of what popular culture calls main character syndrome, a perpetual mindset in which we think the center of our lives is ourselves. While it might not qualify as full-on narcissism, it is an egocentric way to go about life. Also, it's entirely human and smacks of Adam biting the apple and blaming Eve. This way of life is always able to protect the ego by blaming people and circumstances outside of ourselves for our emotional and spiritual state.

There are going to be bullies along the way and, yes, we need to have boundaries, but we can deal with all that from the inside-out as well. I remember being in college when a guy tried to pick a fight with my friend, Dave, in a bar. He was taking ice cubes out of his drink and throwing them at Dave. Obviously, that wasn't acceptable, but Dave didn't want to get in his face and have this escalate. So he walked over to the guy, smiled like he was greeting an old friend who was just messing with him, and bought him a drink. Bullies don't know what to do when their efforts at intimidation are met with friendly confidence and shared joy. Of course, Dave had to forgive him for being a bit of a jerk initially, but that's a lot easier to do when you're living inside-out. The two ended up having a good conversation not just that night, but the next few times we saw him in that bar as well. Turning the other cheek isn't about relinquishing your power; it's about reclaiming your inner power and taking control of the energy that surrounds you. This is, after all, how Jesus lived.

Most of us get up in the morning and go about our day with our attention and concern primarily focused on our own experience. We think about the things we have to do, the places we have to go, and perhaps the people we're going to see. If it involves things we look forward to doing, places we want to go, and people we want to see, we greet the day with joy. But if we must deal with challenging tasks, uncomfortable places, or difficult people, we get a bit of a stomach churn. This is so natural and intuitive we don't even think about it. We aren't even aware that we have a choice.

Living inside-out, as my friends Chris, Dave, and John exemplify, reverses the direction of life's energy. Instead of life happening to us, it happens through us. Rather than evaluating our experiences based on how they affect us, we consider them in terms of how they enable us to positively affect the experiences of others.

It takes a regular spiritual practice to train ourselves to live from the inside-out. Arguably, that's a big part of what spirituality is ultimately about—developing the life habit of living from the heart and soul, more concerned with the good we're putting in the world than the experience we're getting from the world. Once we reach that point, we are finally ready to open ourselves to meaning and purpose. This is the flex point where we are ready to pivot from merely doing stuff to living with vocation.

8

The I Am Question

MATT AND HIS COLLEAGUES SAT STIFFLY IN A CONFER- ENCE ROOM. The men wore coats and ties; the few women (three, to be exact) wore skirts and jackets. It was formal to the point of intimidating, considering this was a man- ufacturing company serving the construction industry in the mid-2000s. It wasn't Wall Street in the 1980s, where pinstripes and wingtips were expected. One would have anticipated polos and khakis or at least a few open col- lars. But this was a conservative, traditional work culture in North Dakota, and they weren't about to change "just because some longhairs in Seattle want to wear flip-flops to work." At least that was how it was explained to Matt in advance of the meeting.

Also explained to him was that there would be people in the room who didn't trust him and his companions. "Just so you're aware," Paul, the VP of Sales and Marketing, had forewarned over drinks the night before, "there are mem- bers of the executive team who don't like you, don't trust you, and don't want you here." He said it as he swirled ice cubes in a glass of scotch. They were sitting in a dimly lit hotel lounge surrounded by head mounts of elk, deer, and other wild game. The whole scene felt like a mid-century movie set.

"But they haven't even met us yet," Matt offered. He was young, just scratching the front side of his mid-thirties, and hadn't yet learned to read the context and subtext of these sorts of situations. While others of his generation were raised on cynicism, Matt was a pie-eyed optimist who believed people are objective and prefer reason over emotion.

Paul was twenty years his senior, and he was remarkable in his willingness to take the young man under his wing and coach up his naivete. "Here's the thing," he said patiently, "it will help if you understand where they're coming from—they don't like you and they don't trust you because they think you're from out east, and they don't like or trust anyone from out east who comes here and tells them how to do things."

Sammi, Carol, and Matt all laughed without squinting their eyes, the way people do to mask nervousness. Sammi and Carol were the other two members of the account team who had made the trip, and they would be two of the three women in the room the next day. Carol broke the awkwardness, "But we're not from out east, we're from Illinois, which is as Midwestern as you can get outside of Iowa."

"It's the same neighborhood as North Dakota," Sammi added.

"It doesn't matter," Paul said. "You're from east of the Mississippi, so as far as they're concerned, you might as well be from Boston or New York. This is a rugged DIY culture out here, and they're convinced they can figure out just about everything on their own, because mostly they have. So, there will be a few folks at the table with a chip on their shoulder. Don't take it personally." He set his scotch on the table and lit a cigarette. "David and Sean want you here—they invited you. That's all that matters. We don't have the skills and know-how to market at a high level to a national audience. They know it; they're smart guys. This meeting is intended to win over the naysayers. So just be your charming selves."

Matt had never thought of himself as charming. Just the opposite, actually. He usually felt a bit socially insecure and awkward, so he decided it would be best to camp in the weeds and let Sammi and Carol carry conversations.

David and Sean were the President/CEO and Executive Vice President/COO respectfully. They weren't perfect, but they were grounded and true to their values, prioritizing people over profits. Matt saw them as role models, which didn't ease his discomfort.

When they entered the conference room the next day, the room setup was much more egalitarian than expected. There was no indication of a traditional hierarchical order that is often packaged with such traditional business attire. David sat along one of the sides, erasing any symbolism of power or authority. This was not a formal meeting, even though it certainly felt like one. As Paul had advised, it was intended to be a roundtable conversation, an opportunity for the executive team to get to know this marketing group before they all went to dinner together. David firmly believed the best way to get to know someone is by breaking bread and pouring wine together.

After the initial handshaking and polite banter, David shared a few words of welcome and invited their guests to each give a self-introduction. "Tell us who you are," he said. "Let us get to know you."

Carol was by far the most experienced among the three and had the most impressive credentials, so she stepped up and went first. Sitting confidently with both hands folded on the table, she made terrific eye contact as she ran through her resumé, including her education and career accomplishments, hitting high points that would be most relevant to the people in the room. Matt tried to make himself small, hoping Sammi would go next, because, following Carol, he feared he would look like he belonged at the kids' table and shouldn't be trusted with a fork.

When she finished, David smiled graciously and quickly surveyed the faces in the room. "That was very impressive, Carol. Thank you. You've told us much about what you've done, but we still don't know who you are." He smiled warmly. "The question wasn't about your credentials. We already have confidence in your qualifications. We want to know who you are." He spoke with a soft ease that was meant to be balm for the burn. Still, the room fell silent.

Carol started again. Her voice shook and her neck turned red. David gently interrupted, "It's all good, Carol. You responded very professionally the way everyone everywhere would expect. You'll discover that we're not like everyone everywhere. We'll give you a few minutes to get used to us and come back to you." He turned and looked directly at Matt, "Please show her how it's done, Matt. Tell us who you are."

Matt's throat went dry, and he felt his armpits weeping. Who am I? It's the elusive question most of us spend our entire lives either chasing or avoiding. Is it even answerable? Or is it a horizon that keeps moving as we pursue it?

In the seventh grade, Sister Mary Carlita had asked him to write an essay on this very same topic. It struck Matt that here he was, a fully grown man in a suit with a family and a mortgage, and he was less sure of his answer than when he was thirteen. He was terrified and wanted to slide under the table, but vulnerability is a sun that casts no shadow. Its heat refuses to be obstructed by objects and structures, yet we keep cowering behind artificial facades and self-illusions, hoping to hide the truth about ourselves. Matt found himself alone on a stage with no curtain, living a naked-in-public dream he wished he could wake from.

"I am..." he started, and then paused, feigning thoughtful introspection while mustering courage to continue. Looking for a handle to grasp, his eye caught Carol. She was still recovering, and he calculated that the risk of not being purely authentic at this point was greater than the risk of vulnerability. He restarted, this time surrendering to the flow. "I am...still trying to decide what I want to be when I grow up—but I haven't yet figured out what it even means to grow up, and there is a part of me that secretly hopes I won't have to. So I keep kicking that can down the road. Somehow, I stumbled into marketing as a copywriter, which is a great place for someone who wants to learn everything but not settle exclusively on anything.

"I am a husband and a father of a shy son and a precocious daughter whom I sometimes wish would reel it in, but I'm glad she doesn't. I am trying to be a good dad and good husband, but I'm not sure I always am. In fact, I'm quite sure I'm not, so I keep working at getting better. Most days, I'm baffled as to why God would trust me to raise children, which causes me to question my Creator's judgment.

"I am a lot of things, I suppose—a youth baseball coach, the son of two teachers, an avid reader—but I am not really a suit and tie guy. This is not my natural habitat and I'm finding it difficult to pretend I'm comfortable in this moment. I'm more of a jeans and work boots guy who would be much more at home trudging through a forest or tying flies. Mostly, I'm a wannabe cowboy poet who hopes to put some good into this world as long as I'm in it anyway."

And then he stopped. After a silent moment, he shrugged his shoulders to indicate he was finished. It's an awkward thing to have a monologue without a conclusion, but awkwardness, he decided, was a part of his authenticity, so it somehow felt natural.

Later, David made sure he sat next to Matt at dinner because, "You strike me as a thinker," he said.

Authenticity may be relatively safe when we're alone at home scribbling in a journal, but on display in public for all the world to see, it can be one of the scariest things we do. Until we've done it. Once we have dropped all the masks and let the world see that we are naked pilgrims on a winding journey who get pelted by rain and hail, pounded by wind, and scorched by the hot sun, then—and not until then—are we truly free to live with meaning and pursue purpose.

Unless we take this plunge into the deep waters of vulnerability, we will be held captive by our ego's notion that creation came into its fullness the moment we showed up and did the world a favor by drawing some of its air into our precious lungs. Regardless of what our mothers might have told us, all of creation up to the moment of our birth was not preparation for our arrival. We are mere passersby, small clumps of stardust blowing through this earthly realm for a moment. While the thought of that bludgeons us with vulnerability, it also blesses us with freedom.

> Who am I? It's the elusive question most of us spend our entire lives either chasing or avoiding.

We don't realize it, but our vulnerability is a gift that relieves us of the pressure to be perfect. We can be scraped, scarred, clumsy, bruised, and awkward and still be lovable. We can be stumbling, bumbling, flailing, failing, and ailing castoffs on the Island of Misfit Toys and still be created in God's own image and likeness. Vulnerability, like Jesus on the cross, is what love looks like, and it is beautiful. So when we hide our vulnerability, we hide our Christlikeness.

Many of us are raised with a shadow-side duet singing in our minds. One voice tells us we will be more loved (and less vulnerable) if we are admired by others, so we ought to try to impress. The harmonizing voice tells us we become less loveable (and more vulnerable) when we are judged harshly by others. The combination is over-powering. Without even realizing it, we evaluate our own self-worth through the eyes of others, shaping our image to gain affirmation and avoid judgment. Socially, it makes sense to us. Spiritually, it is a train wreck. Instead of dis-covering, nurturing, and sharing the person God created us to be (our authentic self), we become enamored with the image of who we think others want us to be (our false self). Living with a real sense of deep purpose and mean-ing is nearly impossible if we are not first and foremost authentic and honest when reflecting on the question, *who am I?* This means allowing the people at church to see us as broken and imperfect, allowing the people at work to see us as spiritual seekers who take wrong turns, and allowing our children and grandchildren to see us as sometimes lost and confused with more questions than answers.

This brings us back to our earlier discussion about the order of things. Vocation comes forth from identity; iden-tity does not come from vocation. Our awareness and understanding of how we each answer *who am I* is a pre-requisite to a life of meaning and purpose, even though we spend much of life building this plane while flying it. Ultimately, our pilgrimage through this very brief lifetime can awaken within us a deep awareness of our true, authen-tic identity—I am a living, breathing creation made in the image and likeness of the infinite I AM; I am an expres-sion of love given life by the One who is love. When that happens, we are truly ready to begin living with meaning, purpose, and vocation.

As I walked with the *who am I* question on retreat, pondering the peaceful majesty of great oaks and maples that have stood their ground, rooted in their creation far longer than I have, it occurred to me that all of creation exists in harmony, yet somehow so many humans live in disharmony. The oak doesn't need to be affirmed in its oakness, nor does the lichen need to be validated in its lichenness. The squirrel has no need to be as beautiful as the butterfly, and the bullfrog does not get jealous of the water lily. All of creation is simply sacred as it is. How is it that only we humans, created in God's image and likeness, struggle with and even fight over our identity?

At that point, I paused, sat in the dirt under a tree, and breathed in a deep awareness that I, even more so than the oak and the maple, got my identity exclusively from the Creator. There is nothing I could or should do to try to improve on it, or to attempt to re-create myself in any image that is not of God. And that image is the very likeness of unconditional love, unlimited joy, and unqualified mercy.

I am one with the I AM. And what more could I possibly hope to become? What more is there? This alone is the identity I am called to bring from the inside-out to my very brief role as husband, father, businessperson, writer, deacon, and homeless advocate. This is what gives meaning to every breath, gives purpose to my every minute, and gives vocation to my every effort.

9

To Live with Meaning Is to Live Authentically

LUCIA BREATHED DEEPLY AND SAT STRAIGHT WHILE HOPING TO LOOK RELAXED. "Zoom interviews can be so mechanical and dehumanizing," she thought to herself. "They may be convenient, but they're soulless."

On the other end, three interviewers sat under florescent lights at least ten feet from a camera purchased by someone whose bonus hinged on saving money. Either that or this company had been extremely forward-thinking with technology sixteen years ago and saw no need to upgrade a camera that still worked, at least sort of. The image was both grainy and blurry, like a home movie on VHS. One of the interviewers appeared to be cleaning his fingernails, but it was hard to tell. Lucia imagined that an up-close image of her own face was splashing across an eighty-inch HD screen. They would have upgraded the image they viewed but, like most of us, wouldn't have considered how others view things.

One of the interviewers, Lilah, asked most of the questions. The others took notes or doodled grocery lists; there was no way of knowing. Lilah stuck to a script of preordained, officially approved and sanctioned interview questions, never deviating or riffing off Lucia's answers. Process seemed to matter more than content, procedure more than authenticity. If anyone was going to bring human warmth and joy to this conversation, it would have to be Lucia herself, but how do you do that through a video conference when you're outnumbered three to one and you can't read the expressions on anyone's face?

The first few questions were general pablum: Tell us about yourself, Lucia. What inspired you to apply for a position with our company? Why do you think you would be a good fit for this position? Then came the round of specific pablum: How would you describe your time management skills? What are your goals? Where do you see yourself in five years?

Yawn. Interview questions are so often predictably shallow and rehearsed. The answers are likewise shallow and rehearsed. The thought occurred to Lucia that most first-round job interviews are little more than mannequins playing ping-pong. If you win at being plastic, you get upvoted to a room with someone interested in your humanity. Maybe. In that moment she decided, come what may, she would play in her own flesh and blood. Her responses would not be woven from synthetic fibers and arranged by a stylist. They'd have texture like the earth itself. They'd be as real as dirt, as honest as mulch, and as innocent as seedlings.

"Time management? I don't concern myself with it much. Time is God's realm. I'm just here to use whatever time I'm given to put some good in the world." Lucia giggled silently to herself before doubling down and expanding, "No one who has done anything great went down in history for their time management skills. Martin Luther King is remembered for his content and his character, not for his conciseness. Shakespeare may have been prolific, but no one cares if he was efficient. And Jesus, well c'mon, he was always wandering off into the wilderness or the garden or somewhere. No one knows if Jesus had time management skills, and no one cares." She was on a surprising roll, and no one was stopping her, so she just kept going. "It's not that managing time isn't important to me, it's just not a priority. I'd rather manage my mind, my heart, and my energy. Sometimes I get lost in thought and it's the most productive time I spend."

Even through the blurry, low-res image, Lucia could make out blank faces. Lilah looked down at her papers. The fingernail guy stared at the screen as though deciphering a language he didn't speak. Lucia knew she had thrown a pie into the clown face of protocol, but it felt so good, so freeing. She might be blowing up the interview, but she was being real and authentic, without concern for an expected script. Inside, she knew that time management is a valid concern in any organization, but everyone professes to be good at it, and even if they are, what's the point of being efficient with mediocre work? The next question did not go better.

"My goals? I'm not entirely sure I believe in goals. I think life is more about living in the moment and making a difference where you are. I guess my only goal is to share my talents and my character in a way that makes the world a little better. If I can do that, I think I will have accomplished something valuable." Lucia was intentional about conveying joy in her voice. She smiled broadly when she spoke, and she surprised herself at the honest hubris of her own answers. As much as she wanted to humanize the exchange, she had no idea if her personality was being received on the other end or if she was just coming across as a smart-aleck punk who lacks a firm grip on reality. Nonetheless, pens were moving. Notes were being scratched.

Having gone this deep into authentic honesty, Lucia just dove straight into the next question. "In five years—I have no idea where I'll be. Wherever the whispers of spirit nudge me, I guess. I just believe the life breath of the Spirit will lead me to greater happiness and fulfillment than I could find on my own, so I've just decided to follow that voice."

Silence.

More silence.

It was a very honest answer, authentic to the core. Lilah finally raised her eyes and ad-libbed, "So what do you envision that looking like in five years?"

"I have no idea," Lucia confessed. "The Spirit has an imagination far greater than mine, so I don't want to limit the possibilities by imposing my own narrow vision."

Two days later Lucia received an email informing her that while they were very impressed with her qualifications and credentials, they had decided to move forward with other candidates. However, they certainly enjoyed meeting her and would keep her resume on file for future reference should a suitable position become available.

There was nothing authentic about that correspondence. It was, Lucia thought, BS spun like cotton candy.

When you ask organizational leaders what they really need in future employees, they'll list things such as *a big picture understanding of how things work together, the ability to bring vision and imagination to the job, open-mindedness,* and *out-of-the-box problem solving skills.* This is true whether you're talking about business, health care, education, government, military, or even religion. Leaders across the board lament a perceived shortage of people who set their own egos and self-interests aside to serve a good greater than the self. Whether we're talking about a chief financial officer or the volunteer who calls bingo numbers at the senior center, we all want to spend our days alongside well-adjusted, joyful, and inspired people who bring a developed combination of personality, humanity, imagination, and spirituality to their work every day. That's more important to us in a teammate than unabashed career ambition, yet we rarely and barely screen for these things when considering candidates. We're more comfortable with people who signal that they'll contort to fit the mold we cast (created in our image) than people who dare to let us see who they authentically are (created in God's image). And yet, once we get to know who someone authentically is, we can't get enough. These are the people we most trust.

Simultaneously, we all want to be that person. Right? We all want to be well-adjusted, joyful, and inspired people with vision beyond the tip of our own nose. We want to think of ourselves as imaginative people who set ego aside and serve a good greater than the self, people who bring a developed combination of personality, humanity, and grounded spirituality to whatever we do. Well, maybe we don't all want that, but, scoundrels and psychopaths aside, most of us do.

Somehow, though, there often is a gap between how we want to self-identify and how we live. I want to be giving, but I'm often selfish. I want to be compassionate, but I'm often judgmental. I want to be peaceful, but I'm often anxious. The list of contrasts goes on. A great portion of our adult lives is spent wrestling with the stress caused by this gap. It perplexes us, yet few of us are aware that we're the ones who put it there. We create the gap through our own internal disharmony. It's a choice we make without even realizing we're making it.

Using the language of our ancestors, I suppose we could think of it as a form of original sin—the idea that we all inevitably live in the gap between our spiritual authenticity and the daily grind of life. For example, my wife, Michelle, loves me in the depths of her beautiful soul. Her spiritual intention is to live in loving harmony with me. But when I track dirt across her freshly washed floor, she wants to scream me out of her life. Thus, the daily grind of life stirs an emotional response that conflicts with her desire for a calm, centered spirit. Thankfully, Michelle has figured out how to reconcile that tension, and most often she chooses to center on her intention (forgiving love) rather than react to her understandable frustration. She lives from the inside-out. I am blessed.

Simultaneously, my spiritual intention is to live in peaceful harmony with Michelle as well. So why would I track dirt into the house in the first place if I know it bothers her? Well, because in the daily grind of life I sometimes lose connection with my spiritual intention, and I don't think beyond the tip of my nose. People who know us both like her better. Obviously.

This gap between spiritual intention and daily living is more easily seen at the community and corporate level, perhaps because we needn't be self-reflective when observing it. We tend to see more objectively when observing people, relationships, and organizations that aren't personal. Institutions that state one thing in their missions and then make decisions that seem the exact opposite are nearly cliché. We could easily go on *ad nauseum* with examples of hypocrisies in government, business, religion, education, and every other institution, but such is not our point here. Besides, that fruit hangs so low it hits us in the head. It's too easy.

We would be wise to step back, hitch up our self-awareness britches, and admit something to ourselves: all the human institutions we readily complain about are merely aggregations of the people who comprise them, so it should come as no surprise that they are rife with dissonance and hypocrisies. We—all of us—live with chronic dissonance. We say we want one thing, but our choices and actions would suggest something else. We are remarkably self-contradictory.

It is very difficult to authentically live from the inside-out when we lie to ourselves or when we bend reason and tint our lenses to avoid confronting our own contradictions. When I was a kid during the Cold War, Sister Felix Marie used to start each class by making us all pray for the end of tyranny, and then she'd smack us upside the head with her bible if we stepped out of line. Her cringeworthy joke was, "Maybe the word of God can knock some sense into you." As a teacher, she was a tyrant who taught us to live in fear of her wrath. This might seem like an extreme or one-off example, but we often repeat this same pattern in the way we run our businesses, families, and even our religions. From parents threatening (or even delivering) emotional or physical abuse upon misbehaving children, to pastors who tell congregants they'll go to hell for their transgressions, we use fear as a tool to manipulate and control the behaviors of others. Of course, this causes stress and anxiety! That's exactly what fear is designed to do. Yet we profess belief in a Christ who repeatedly said *fear not, peace be with you, and love one another.* Certainly, I cannot be the only one who sees the dissonance in this. Our own attitudes and behaviors are at odds with our beliefs. It is a fool's errand to pursue meaning, purpose, and vocation when we are so out of sync within ourselves.

We say we want hope, but we engage in endless conversations about everything we think is wrong with the world and spend very little time in conversation about all the good in the world. We say we want joy, but we complain about everything from the price of gas to the way the neighbor takes care of their lawn. I'm perplexed by

LIVE LIKE YOU MEAN IT

coworkers who gripe about all that's wrong with everyone else, and then complain about low morale in the workplace. It doesn't occur to them that they've become the principal agents of the low morale. That's the dissonance between how we want to live (happiness) and the way we choose to live (focused on unhappiness).

It is very difficult to authentically live from the inside-out when we lie to ourselves...

We all do it, yet most of us never see it. It's as though our brains, hearts, and souls barely nod to each other when passing in the corridor, much less sit down in the same room together and find their common story. This is an important dynamic a regular religious practice ought to foster but somehow seldom does.

On a flight from Seattle to Minneapolis, I was sitting next to a woman named Sarah, from Yakima, who wore a delicate gold necklace with a small diamond embedded in the center of a cross. Somewhere over Montana, the aircraft's Wi-Fi glitched, and a flight attendant announced they would need to reboot. They were "very sorry for the inconvenience. It should take only about five minutes. Thank you for your patience." "Huh," I thought. "We're cruising above the clouds at 535 miles per hour and I'll be on the ground in time for lunch. What possible inconvenience are they apologizing for? That I need to wait five minutes before resuming season two, episode four of *Ted Lasso*, which I'm watching for the third time, anyway?"

I pulled off my headset and glanced over toward the window, making incidental eye contact with Sarah. Being from the Midwest, I smiled politely. That's just our way. Yakima Sarah jumped into the opening, "This is why I never fly Delta."

I smiled again, although this time with more confusion.

"It's always something," she said. "I mean, even Walmart has Wi-Fi that works. It's not hard, people. For what they charge for these seats, is that too much to ask?"

Since I had already been splattered by her splash, I decided to jump into the pool, albeit facetiously. "They just don't make airplanes like they used to, do they? Twenty years ago, jets flew all over the world and the Wi-Fi never glitched."

Yakima Sara was eager to agree but missed the sarcasm, "Isn't that the truth! Everything has gotten so complicated. People just expect so much these days."

I wondered who these *people* who *expect so much* are. Does it include people who expect Wi-Fi on an airplane? For a moment I considered asking her, but that moment passed quickly. "On the bright side," I offered instead, "none of us will die of dysentery as we make our way across the country."

"I guess that's true. We should all be a bit more grateful for what we have, I suppose," she paused and seemed to ponder momentarily. "People without gratitude end up feeling so entitled. That's a big part of the problem with America today. Everyone feels so self-entitled."

Again, I wondered who the *people* are that she was talking about. Who is the *everyone* who feels so *entitled*? I smiled, this time raising my eyebrows slightly.

At the beginning of this book, I invited you to choose possibility over problems. Doing so is integral to understanding purpose and meaning in life. See, God created empowering things like love, peace, joy, mercy, compassion, and justice. These are the things that create possibility and give promise to the world. To live authentically is to believe in them and to let your life be shaped by them from the inside-out. Humanity created power structures such as governments, economies, corporations, nation states, and institutional hierarchies. All these things can be used for good or evil, and I'm not suggesting for a moment that they don't have value. They can, do, and should. But they're not of God. If you place your faith in them, you can and will be let down. It's inevitable. As human creations, they are all flawed, and those flaws will be exposed.

Living a life of meaning only happens when we choose empowerment over power. The dynamics of power are tempting, a real ego boost and head rush; and sources of power in our culture are readily available—wealth, position, beauty, personality, etc. Ultimately, though, they are empty. Power is illusionary, a false god. We cannot hold it because the only source of any real power is God's own self, the source of all life and love. Anyone who thought they were on top of the world only to be stricken with cancer or wiped out in a climate event knows this.

Healthy empowerment, in contrast, makes us channels for love, joy, mercy, peace, gratitude, and all good things that come from God and change the world for the better. Think of empowerment as the way God works in the world through us. We are empowered by God, a reality that is deeply meaningful.

I am not the source of power.

I am an empowered channel for God to work in the world.

10

Vocation
of the Moment

FOR OVER FORTY YEARS, MY MOTHER PACKED MY FATHER'S LUNCH EVERY MORNING. She got up early, made several sandwiches, packed fruit and cookies, and even scooped ice cream into a cold thermos bottle. She did this five, sometimes six, days a week, every week, for over forty years. And she found it tedious, boring, and more than mildly unfulfilling. Yet she did it. Again. And again. And again.

When I was home visiting at one point, she confided how she secretly hated doing it. In fact, there was part of her that resented it, and she couldn't wait for my dad to retire so she would be free from this daily chore. She might have used language a little more colorful than that. My mom is a poet. It's a gift passed to her from her own father who had this remarkable ability to speak truth in a cut-through way without leaning on vulgarities.

"So why do you do it?" I asked.

"Well, someone has to do it," my mom said. "I mean, your father needs to eat." My mother was quite progressive in her attitude toward gender roles, but when applied to her own marriage, she was tried-and-true traditional. In this regard, what she taught her children departed from how she, herself, lived.

"You know, I had to eat too, when I was growing up, but you made me pack my own lunch."

"I was doing a favor for your future wife. I was teaching you to be responsible for yourself so she could be free from the drudgery of having to do it for you."

"Do you really think Michelle would feel compelled to pack my lunch for me if I didn't manage it myself? Do you think she would stand for that?"

"I would certainly hope not! But these are different times than when your dad and I were first married."

"Right. They are different times. And need I remind you that you and Dad live in these times right along with the rest of us?" This is how the relationship between my mother and me had been since I was twelve years old. We logic sparred. She would never accept the lame and manipulative logic of a teenage boy, and she relentlessly challenged me to think deeper and more cohesively. She knew my fragile junior high ego would not allow me to be bested by a five-foot two-inch middle-aged mom, and she used it with blackbelt savvy to leverage my own momentum against myself. Thirty years had passed since then, and I had learned to duel with a blade nearly as keen as hers.

"So what would happen if you stopped packing Dad's lunch every day?" In asking the question, I knew very well that I might as well have been asking what would happen if birds suddenly quit flying or fish decided swimming all day was too tedious so they would merely float instead. For my mom, packing Dad's lunch was no more a choice she made than was baking her own bread or even breathing for that matter. It was in her nature.

"Oh, that would never happen," she retorted quickly. "I mean, I can't imagine. The sun would probably fall out of the sky and all the stars in the heavens would implode."

"Ahh, so you can't stop yourself? You have no power over this?"

"Well," she paused at the counter in the kitchen and set down her knife. "I guess I don't want to stop. I do it because I love him."

There it was. Packing Dad's lunch every morning—the endless routine of getting up early, brewing coffee, and making sandwiches—was not about the lunch at all. It was about the love. This was eucharistic for my mom. It was one of the ways she broke herself open and poured herself out in love for my father.

We don't think of the little things as vocational. We don't think of the moments, the tedium, and the relatively mindless daily routines as expressions of purpose or flashes of meaning. When my mother thought about packing Dad's lunch from the outside-in, as a burden assigned for her to carry, she resented it. But when she reversed the direction of her mindful flow and thought of it from the inside-out as a daily expression of love, she gave herself to it freely, willingly, and even gratefully.

Before enlightenment, according to the Zen saying, chop wood and carry water. After enlightenment, chop wood and carry water. The difference isn't in what we do; it's in the mind with which we do it. "Do small things with great love," Saint Theresa of Calcutta advised. This is where life has meaning. Two people can do the exact same thing, and while one finds it boring and tedious, the other finds it to be rewarding. In fact, the same person can do the same thing on two different days and find it enriching one day but soul-draining the next day. What gives? The difference is not in the thing being done, the way it is done, or the preference of the person doing it. The difference is in the heart, mind, and soul with which we approach the task.

From this perspective, we begin to understand that vocation isn't necessarily about life's work; it is often about the moment's work. For the new father, vocation can be as immediate as changing a diaper. In that moment, he is directing the time and the love he has been given in his own life toward the benefit of another person. It might be unpleasant and even brutally disgusting at times, but it is profoundly meaningful, purposeful, and vocational if he sees it as an opportunity to break himself open and pour himself out in loving service to the child. You can roll your eyes at me if you wish, but you know this is universally true.

When I was much younger and building homes with my father, I hated roofing. This wasn't a mild distaste. It was a seething and loathsome resentment. And I lacked the maturity and wisdom to keep it to myself. Instead, I openly grumbled and complained, making sure everyone around me could share a piece of my misery.

One morning my father took me aside. "You know, your attitude makes it worse."

I was in no mood for a life lesson about my disposition, so I pretended to ignore him while I mumbled, "Nothing can make this worse." But he heard me.

Stepping closer, he looked me in the eye and said, "The house needs a roof. We're not going to build a house without a roof, so you might as well suck it up and do it with a smile because you're going to have to do it either way."

He was right, of course. But he wasn't done. What followed was life-shaping wisdom from a carpenter who knew a thing or two about grit. "You're thinking about the wrong thing," he continued. "You're thinking about the work you must do that you don't want to do. But you can choose to think about something more important—think about the people who are going to live in this house, about kids being tucked into bed at night under the security of this roof. They need a home that keeps them warm and dry. That's what you're doing today."

My father completely reframed roofing. He gave it purpose and made it a vocation—an effort undertaken for the benefit of others—and he gave me a reason to take pride in the work. Even more so, he taught me about embracing what I now call the vocation of the moment. When thinking about the key to a life filled with meaning and joy, a vocation of the moment may unlock far more than a vocation of a lifetime.

We can all live this way every moment of every day if we choose. In fact, it is the inevitable manifestation of a contemplative life rich in prayer. Our vocation of the moment draws us into a mindful awareness of the sacredness of life right now and the effect we are having on the people and creation around us. It asks us to bring our intention to the fore, and in doing so it teaches us to live from the inside-out. I am wholly convinced that we experience deep, meaningful spiritual growth each time we move our focus from task to mission, from *what* to *why*. This is equally true whether I am in the process of shoveling snow from my neighbor's driveway or cleaning my

We don't think of the little things as vocational. We don't think of the moments, the tedium, and the relatively mindless daily routines as expressions of purpose or flashes of meaning.

bathroom. Even when walking in the woods, if I focus on my vocation of the moment—to surrender ego and become one with creation—I emerge into a deeper spirituality, increasingly aware that each breath is a gift reminding me that life isn't here to serve me; I am here to serve it.

A group of women at my church knit prayer shawls for the sick and blankets for the newly baptized. They do it with faith because seldom are they present when these items are given to a cancer patient or to a frazzled and overwhelmed new mom. They're not in the room when someone is wrapped in the fruits of their labors. What's in it for them, some would ask. Why do they use their limited resources to purchase yarn? Why do they spend so many hours of a waning lifetime doing something from which they receive no benefit? Why do they grind gnarled and arthritic hands to the point of exhaustion to knit something for someone they'll never even know, someone who will never know they did it? They are sowing seeds for a harvest they will never reap, and in the wisdom of their life stage they have discovered that meaning is not something we get from life; it's something we bring to life.

Also from S. JAMES MEYER

Living with Real Presence
Eucharist as an Approach to Life

In this transformative book, S. James Meyer introduces us to a whole-life encounter with the living Christ, awakening a fresh awareness that the Eucharist is about life, love, and relationship. A spiritual journey for personal reflection or small-group discussion, *Living with Real Presence* reminds us that our lives, Christ's life, and all lives are united in a sacred communion with our Creator and creation.

128 PAGES | **$14.95** | **5½" X 8½"** | **9781627857185**

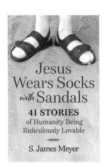

Jesus Wears Socks with Sandals
41 Stories of Humanity Being Ridiculously Lovable

With joyful depth, compelling style, and wry humor, *Jesus Wears Socks with Sandals* shines a light on just how near and clear Christ is in our ordinary encounters with life. S. James Meyer offers another bridge-building book packed with fodder for meaningful conversations between people of all faith levels and perspectives.

128 PAGES | **$14.95** | **5½" X 8½"** | **9781627855587**

God Plays a Purple Banjo
and 41 Other Stories of Inspiration, Hope, and Humor

This refreshing, delightfully written, and deeply personal book provides the answer to the age-old question, "Where is God?" Everywhere, says S. James Meyer. Each of the stories here uses the stuff of everyday life to remind us that every breath we take is an encounter with God, and that there is no moment in our lives that is not sacred.

128 PAGES | **$14.95** | **5½" X 8½"** | **9781627854429**

TO ORDER CALL 1-800-321-0411 |  **TWENTY-THIRD**
OR VISIT WWW.TWENTYTHIRDPUBLICATIONS.COM | **PUBLICATIONS**
A division of Bayard, Inc.